voices of
Chalford, Bisley
and Bussage

Tempus ORAL HISTORY *Series*

voices of
Chalford, Bisley
and Bussage

Tamsin Treverton Jones

TEMPUS

Frontispiece: *Frankie Gardiner with his donkey on Rack Hill.*
(Photograph courtesy of Peckham's, Stroud)

First published 2004

Tempus Publishing Limited
The Mill, Brimscombe Port,
Stroud, Gloucestershire, GL5 2QG

www.tempus-publishing.com

British Library Cataloguing in Publication Data.
A catalogue record for this book is available from the British Library.

ISBN 0 7524 3204 4

Typesetting and origination by Tempus Publishing Limited
Printed in Great Britain by Midway Colour Print, Wiltshire

Contents

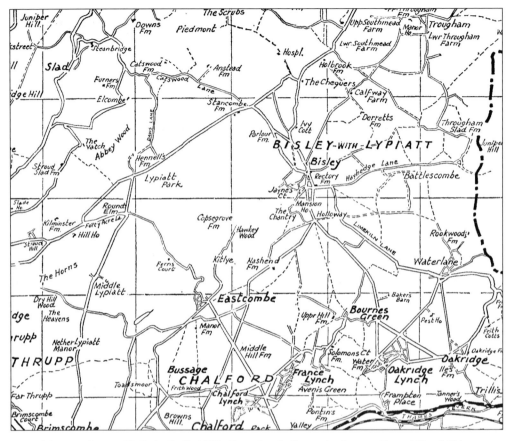

Map of the area, showing Chalford, Chalford Hill, France Lynch, Eastcombe, Bussage, Brownshill and Bisley.

Foreword

I felt a combination of elation and terror when we first arrived. It was like getting to the South Pole really, and landing there. One was assaulted by the beauty: the yellow stone that blazes in any light. This is an adorable village, a civilised and lovely village. It's almost as if the houses can't get enough of each other, it's as if they are having a terrific gossip and they're all falling over each other. There are all sorts of people here: you can go out on any day and have the most fantastic conversation, from Proust to pumpkins.

Jilly Cooper (Bisley)

My first introduction to the village was through the British Legion, because I had been a soldier. I went via the pub, which a friend of mine had recommended – it was known then as the Stomach Pump. The landlord was Les Restall, who was a remarkable character. The hard core of Bisley men were perfectly happy once they realised I'd been a soldier, played a bit of cricket and wasn't averse to the odd pint of beer.

Leo Cooper (Bisley)

Introduction

'You've got to start with Rosie Franklin,' Vanessa, the Chalford postmistress told me. Of course, I know Rosie, she's a familiar local figure, walking everywhere with her rucksack. Rosie has always lived in the same cottage and if anyone could tell me about life in Chalford, she could. So that's where I started. I was not disappointed. She spoke to me in great detail about growing up in the valley, about childhood games, local characters and about a way of life now gone.

Chalford, Chalford Hill, France Lynch, Eastcombe, Bussage, Brownshill and Bisley: a sense of community used to run like a fine thread through these villages. Each has its own separate and distinct personality, defined by its location, its church and its inhabitants – all, nevertheless, connected to each other by a network of footpaths and donkey tracks. Like Rosie, everyone walked everywhere: from the top of the hill to the bottom and back up again. The only way to get to Oakridge was to walk; the only way up Coppice Hill was on foot; you could only go courting in Bisley if you went for a walk, after church, along the Chalford road and back. That's how it was done, that's how people met, swapped stories, fell in love, built their communities. The 'bustling High Street' fed and clothed these people as they went about their daily business.

Public transport played its part in bringing people together too. Yvonne Crew told me, 'If you could get to Chalford, you could get anywhere' and it was true: the famous Chalford Railcar ran people along the valley to Stroud and Stonehouse, and they all remember it. Pam Turner recalls knitting 'pounds and pounds of wool' on the railcar and Jean Tanner remembers the name of every person who stood on Chalford station with her, at the same time each morning.

Those who delivered life's basics became central characters in these communities: familiar and friendly figures whose arrival every day at the same time, with freshly-baked bread or pails of milk, was a reassuring, even life-affirming presence – as well as a chance to talk and catch up with any news. Harry Cadwallader started out as the bread boy before becoming Chalford's beloved milkman and devoting his working life to serving his community. When we talked, his affection for those he'd served shone out of him, and when he retired after thirty-two years with the milk crate, tributes to him were fulsome and genuine and his story even made the national press!

I was not prepared, however, for the darker details: when she was only five months old, Rosie was adopted by an elderly couple and strict, religious fervour dominated her young life. Although her experiences are quite unique, I began to find, as I networked my way through the valley and up the hill, that nobody's life was untouched by sadness or difficulty, by poverty or hardship – that times were indeed harder then.

Chapter 1, 'A Start in Life', tells astonishing stories of abandonment, adoption and death for which nowadays, no doubt, we would offer counselling and group therapy. Yet I found no self-pity, just acceptance.

There are those now who are determined, in their own way, to keep the spirit of their villages alive: Hilda, Gwen and Phyllis go to every single jumble or cake sale in Bisley and never miss Ascension Day. Michael Mills has been the keeper of the extraordinary Gardiner/Padin collection of photographs, documenting the changes to Chalford and the valleys over the last century. He regularly gives talks and slide shows – lest we forget. George Gleed has written down his magical memories, and Michael Tanner captivates with the sheer eloquence of his testimony.

By making time to tell me their stories, these people have been making history. Not the broad, textbook sweep of history, but more simply how these Cotswold villages evolved, with the church at their centre and a community which helped each other through good times and bad.

We barely hold on to the fragile threads of that community today, as we drive alone in our cars at speed through lanes made for donkey carts. The massive development of the Manor Farm Estate at Bussage has brought new faces and opportunities to the area; its growth has unquestionably diluted the old close-knit society of friends and families, although it is busy forging a new one of its own.

The contributors to this book have helped towards a further understanding of life in Bisley, Chalford and the hilltop villages as it used to be and, perhaps, never can be again. I so enjoyed meeting them all and I think – I hope – that they enjoyed re-living their memories for me and my microphone.

Tamsin Treverton Jones

Acknowledgements

Many people have helped with this book: those I have interviewed have not only been generous with their words and their time, but also with their photographs.

I am grateful to many others who have also helped in different ways:

Joyce Ball, Howard Beard, Jean and Charles Bellamy, Peta Bunbury, R. Clarke, Rita Collins, Leo and Jilly Cooper, John Fendley and the Gloucestershire Catholic History Society, Mike Fenton (*British Railway Journal*), Ian and Katie Jarvis, Susan Maxwell, Pam Perry, Sylvia Watkins, Mark Watson and Judy Wright.

With special thanks to Michael Mills for his unfailing help with photographs and to David Buxton and Matilda Pearce at Tempus for their advice and support.

Finally, to Greg and to Matilda, Kitty and Rufus for inspiring me.

List of Contributors

Brian Beavis, born 1916
Joan Burns, born 1918
Harry Cadwallader, born 1932
Muriel Cadwallader, born 1939
Pam Clissold, born 1933
Peter Clissold, born 1931
David Collins, born 1922
Yvonne Crew, born 1931
Rosie Franklin, born 1948
George Gleed, born 1930
Muriel Hunt, born 1922
Graham Mayo, born 1934
Irene Mayo, born 1903
Gwen Millin, born 1926
Michael Mills, born 1932
Daphne Neville, born 1937
Norman Rogers, born 1913
Hilda Ruther, born 1920
Derek Shergold, born 1928
Mabel Smith, born 1913
Phyllis Smith, born 1916
Jean Tanner, born 1930
Michael Tanner, born 1926
Pam Turner, born 1927
Kathy Watkins, born 1950
Grace Winstone, born 1911
Florence Workman, born 1910

1 A Start in Life

Brought to Bisley

I was born in Newbury, Berkshire. My mother died when I was fifteen months old. My mother's mother couldn't have me because she was eaten up with arthritis, so I was brought to Bisley to live with my father's mother and father, Mr and Mrs William Banyard. We lived in the house next to the lychgate by the church. I was brought up by my grandparents and an auntie, Dorothy Banyard, who was a teacher at Bisley School. My father married again in Berkshire and hence the stepbrothers and sisters: Harold, Alan, Mervyn, Michael, Joy and Clifford. He didn't come back to Bisley straight away. I don't know, you see – we weren't allowed to talk about things with our grandparents very much as children, it was a different age to what it is today. I wish now that I'd asked more questions, but maybe I wouldn't have had any answers. My father used to come down and visit me and, at Christmas, I used to go down there. But mainly I lived with my grandparents.

Muriel Hunt (Bisley)

That's how I came to Chalford

My full name is Rosemary. I hate going under Rosemary, so I go as Rosie. I'm fifty-five. I was born in Crewe and I was adopted, at five months, at Sheffield. I was in a children's home up there and by the grace of God I wasn't shipped off to Australia like a lot of those kids were then; I came straight here. The tale was, that I had to be adopted by a Seventh Day Adventist family. The lady that had me was a very strict Seventh Day Adventist and so whoever adopted me had to be Seventh Day Adventist. There's a church magazine called *The Messenger* and I was advertised in there. There was this bible worker, knew our mum and dad, Mr and Mrs Smith, here in Chalford. Our mum was a very strict Seventh Day Adventist and she talked Dad into becoming one so that they could adopt me. They came up to get me on the train apparently. They were already both quite old: they'd had two stillborn and a miscarriage and then, here I was: a big, bouncy five-month old. It was bit of a shock to them, really!

So, that's how I came to Chalford.

Rosie Franklin (Chalford)

I never knew my father…

I never knew my father. I am the eldest of seven but I didn't have a very good childhood, really. Mum married when I was four and her husband wasn't all that nice to me. My sister Gwen said to Mother once, 'Hilda would like to know who her father is, it's about time she knew' and Mum said, 'Oh I dunno who he was – I forget.' Can you ever imagine anything like that? I heard rumours about who he was, but I wasn't really sure. So my mother married and had six more after me.

Above: *Muriel Hunt (née Banyard) pictured at only a few months old in 1922.*

Left: *Muriel's mother, Caroline Shill, who died when Muriel was only fifteen months old.*

Harry Cadwallader and his sister Eileen Cousins in May 1948.

My mother and I lived with my grand-mother, and I carried on living with her for a while when Mother got married and then I had to go and live with them. We lived opposite the Stirrup Cup – there's a row of four houses and we lived in the second one up, South View. I lived there all my school days; then I went away to service.

Hilda Ruther (Bisley)

The best parents

I was brought to Chalford on the train when I was two years old, to Chalford station. I was an orphan, Church of England, and the person who was in charge of the 'waifs and strays' was Blanche Young, a schoolteacher from France Lynch. She used to find foster parents. Mrs Rachel Greville and Mrs Brazinell used to have these certain boys; it was all boys, basically, that come to Chalford. I came from Wales. I didn't know nothing about me. I never had any contact with my parents whatsoever.

Mrs Greville was a dressmaker, a very old lady, she'd had two children of her own, but they were grown up. Anyway, she died at seventy-eight and I was twelve then, but she said, 'Don't let Harry go back to the orphanage', was what she said to Doris, her daughter.

So, the daughter and her husband brought me on, and that was Bert and Doris Cousins. Their daughter, and my sister, was Eileen Cousins. They brought me up and they were the best parents you could have. My father, Bert Cousins, was a decorator and he worked for Freemans at Camp. They were highly recognized. They worked for all the toffs round Camp, Miserden and down to Cranham.

Harry Cadwallader (Chalford Hill)

13

A widowed mother and grandmother

My name is Christine Pamela but I go by the name of Pamela. I was born in France Lynch in 1927, in a house belonging to my great-grandfather; it was called Primrose Villa then, it's called Dragonara now. Unfortunately, my mother had only been married less than three years and her husband died. We came back down to live with my grandmother, because she was also a widow. So, I was the only daughter of a widowed mother, living with my widowed grandmother – a Victorian grandmother she was too, very strict. But I had a happy life, really. My mother wasn't envious of anybody, she wasn't a bit bitter. She didn't want to re-marry, she said she had one good man and she didn't want another, which I think is sad, really. She was only thirty when he died. I remember when I got to that age, and I thought, 'I can't believe this'. I was lucky, because Mum was a worker and all she had was ten shillings a week pension; she had that from when she was thirty to when she was sixty, and five shillings for me. And when I left school, then, of course she lost the five shillings. I don't know how she managed, really. My grandmother kept us.

Pam Turner née *Skinner (France Lynch)*

Fostered in Eastcombe

My father, William Collins, was born in Quarhouse in 1903. His mum died in childbirth and he was brought to Bussage when he was one day old and lived in virtually the same two houses for the next ninety-one years. My mother, Rena Lawson, was born in London in 1907. She lived in an orphanage in London for the first few years of her life and then she was brought to an orphanage in Eastcombe, St Elizabeth's. The orphanage was run by the Kilburn sisters; the mother orphanage was in Kilburn and she'd started off in the Hackney branch. There were three sisters: Gladys, Margery and Rena and they were left there for a reason we have never been able to find out. The sisters were split up; Gladys and Margery went to Painswick, and a lady in Eastcombe who wasn't altogether nice to her fostered Rena. She was such a pretty little girl that people in the village used to feel sorry for her, because she used to have to clear up and do work before she went to school. One lady gave her a sixpence. She didn't go to the sweet shop and spend it, because she knew the lady in the sweet shop would tell her foster mother she'd been in, so she put it in a wall as she was coming to school. When she went back she couldn't find it – that sixpence is still in the wall somewhere. She went to school at Eastcombe. The headmaster there wanted her to come and live with him and look after his children because she was the best sewer in the school, but her foster mother said 'No, you're going into the mill'.

David Collins (Bussage)

Nearly born in the ambulance

I was born in 1950. I got a twin, a brother, John, who lives at France Lynch and I got two sisters eight years older and they were twins as well. When we were born there was snow on the ground, and the ambulance man was trying to make a name for himself and hoped we'd be born in the van. He drove up Hyde Hill in the snow and got the ambulance stuck and we were nearly born in the ambulance. John was stillborn, but they did manage to revive him. I came home, but John was kept in Tetbury for three months before he was allowed home – he was always very small.

Kathy Watkins (Brownshill)

Pam Turner (née Skinner) as a baby in 1928 in France Lynch.

Twelve girls then two boys

I was born at Fir Tree Cottage and I lived there till I was married at twenty-four. I'm one of fourteen children – twelve girls and two boys. The twelve girls came first and then two boys at the end. They were: Elsie (she died of diphtheria when she was seven), Ivy, Mildred, Doris, Edie, Phyllis, Elsie, Nancy, Nina, Marjorie, Evelyn, Iris, Ronald and Dennis. We only had two bedrooms and an attic and we used to have to sleep three in a bed; there was only about eighteen months between each of us. I slept with two of my other sisters, one older and one younger, and we used to have to fight over who should have to sleep in the middle. We would sleep in a row in a double room. We had two double

beds in the attic and there were three to a bed.

It was pretty hectic. My mother used to make nearly all our clothes and mend all our shoes, and the sewing machine would be going all the evening, after we'd gone to bed. Either that or she was banging away, mending the shoes. Mother did it all. She was a wonderful mother. Her name was Emily and I never seen her get in temper at all, she was always very level-headed. I don't think she ever smacked any of us. She would go, 'Now then my lady, don't you do that, do as I did tell you,' she did go, but never smacked us. She was very patient. She lived till she was ninety-one. My father was a very hard father – he ruled us with a rod of iron; his name was Sydney Percy Hunt. He wasn't beyond hitting us; the least thing we did wrong, we used to get a smack

Some of the lovely Hunt girls from Bisley in around 1923/24. From left to right: Phyllis (moving), Nancy, Doris (the eldest), Marjorie (on knee with doll), Edie, Nina and Elsie

from him. Mother used to go on at him but he was a very hard father. The least thing that we did wrong, up to bed we had to go.

Phyllis Smith (Bisley)

Death on the Railcar

My father, Charlie Winstone, was killed going to work when I was just fourteen. I had left school and I had just started down at Critchley's. My dad had been out of work through the winter, but he managed to get a job at Downfield somewhere. He left home at about half past seven and walked down to get the railcar. He used to say, 'I'd rather be ten minutes early than ten minutes late', and he got down there in plenty of time but the railcar was late. It was the conductor's fault; Mr Taysum was the driver then. Anyway, when they got to the Downfield Halt, he got out to get Mr Taysum his morning paper.

He'd come back in and he wasn't in the railcar properly.

They told Mr Taysum to move the railcar, but he couldn't see my dad under the engine; he was crossing the line to get into the car. That happened on the first morning train, and the girls down at Critchley's kept it from me all day long. At the end of the day, I came up into Brownshill with Mrs Rowberry; she lived next door and she happened to work down there. We went into the shop and post office at Brownshill. Mrs Marshall was there then and she says, 'Oh, is that right what I heard about your father this morning?' I didn't know anything about it and I just burst out into tears. My brother was only ten and he was at school. Mr White, the schoolmaster then, took Mum down to the hospital in Stroud, but gangrene set in and that was it. So I've had to keep home ever since I left school.

Grace Winstone (Eastcombe)

2 Childhood Memories

Gran saves her legs!

Gran was about average height but very fat and homely. She was invariably dressed in dark clothes, which reached her ankles. The toilet, or privy, was at the other end of the garden so, to save her legs, she used to go into the outhouse, or brew-house as it was more often called, often with me trailing along. There she would straddle an old white pail, which was completely enveloped by the dress, and the result would be thrown onto the garden. I expect I was considered too young to take any notice, but I was observant even then.

George Gleed (Brownshill)

Monday is Washing Day

Mother didn't go out to work; running a house in them days was a full-time job. When we came to Chalford there was no water; we had to walk over to Tankards Spring to get drinking water. There was no gas; lighting was oil lamps and candles. Sewage went straight into the river from Meadow Cottages; it was an open sewer, that river running down through there. But they had some lovely trout! For the washing you'd collect rainwater, make a furnace out in the back kitchen – that was a separate building – and you'd light a fire and boil up the water. It was always a competition between the women who would get the first washing out on the line on a Monday morning. Some would wash a handkerchief

on a Sunday night! And, of course, living along Meadow Cottages, I could see all along the Rack Hill.

Norman Rogers (Chalford)

A real larruping

I remember the walking stick being hung up in the kitchen for me to have a beating with. Mother used to say, 'It says in the Bible, spare the rod and spoil the child.' I used to get this walking stick across my backside, or across my back, or anywhere – I had real beatings. I can remember being sent to bed – I slept in the same room as our mum and dad till I got married – and I can remember that door opening and our mother saying to Dad, 'Stan, she needs a belting,' and before he'd got his coat or his cap off, I could hear him coming up them stairs and the door flinging open and the bed clothes coming back and then I'd get a real larruping. I can remember it as if it were yesterday. People used to say to me 'Oh, how wonderful that those people adopted you' but they didn't know what went on behind closed doors, quite honestly. My mum and dad used to physically fight. I used to wake up in the morning and think 'Please Lord, don't let them be rowing,' and I'd listen and if they were rowing, I'd just want to get back under the covers again. And they'd throw things at each other and my mother would say, 'Get the police, get the police!' Then they'd go to church and my

Norman Rogers in 2003. (Photograph by Peta Bunbury)

mother would play the piano and my dad, who was an elder in the church, would be up the front taking the service and they'd just had this terrible row! People didn't realize what went on. He was the dearest, dearest man, he was so lovely. He was a carpenter by trade and he grew up in the village as well. But my mother, she ruled the roost – she was from Thrupp. There you go, you see – she was an outsider!

Rosie Franklin (Chalford)

The cricket fanatic

My father took the bakery over in 1910, the year I was born; he worked terribly hard and it began to grow. I was a very good baby, if I could see my father. My mother used to say 'I could put you in your pram and you would

pat-a-cake for ages just looking at him working'. I absolutely adored him.

My father would stand on the landing stage above the bakery where the flour went in. That landing stage was my downfall, because there was a cricket pitch in the recreation field opposite, and we were warned that if my father saw any of us walking across the cricket pitch in the wrong shoes, we would be punished. He was an ardent cricket fan. Anyway, one day I took a short cut, and as ill luck would have it I turned and I saw him come out of the loft and I knew he'd seen me. He was worried about me damaging the cricket pitch. So when I got home and saw him – he used to go to bed very early, of course, because he used to start work in the middle of the night – he said to me, 'Have you got something to tell me?' I said, 'Yes I know, it's all right, I'm going to bed.' And off I went. We've often laughed about it

Rosie Franklin (née Smith) as Briar Rose in the Chalford Hill School Christmas play in 1958.

afterwards. I went straight off to bed! I knew I'd done wrong and I knew I would be punished. My mother's word and his word were absolute. You obeyed it without any question.

Florence Workman (France Lynch)

It's that man again

When I was a child, I remember my grandfather with his ear to the radio. He was a great fan of ITMA – *It's That Man Again*, Tommy Handley. That kept us going! It was a radio comedy programme. Of course, the accumulator man came on a Monday and you could all sit back and listen, but when ITMA was on, on a Sunday evening, the accumulator would be fading and everybody got a bit nearer to the radio and it would be left with grandfather with his ear up against the radio:

he'd start laughing and we'd all start laughing. Then on Monday, the accumulator man would deliver and we'd all be back to normal. We got it done at Clack's in Stroud; they had a weekly delivery, because everybody had accumulators in those days.

Graham Mayo (Chalford)

Paratroopers and other games

In those days, everybody along the village would play together, and we had this amazing game called 'Paratroopers'. Even the big fellows like Michael Mills would play. Half would go off and hide – it was like glorified hide-and-seek really, but all over the village. It would be as far as the bus stop and probably up the Rack Hill and probably as far as the end of Ashmeads. It used to happen every night. Everybody used to gather in the park and just go and we would play it for hours and hours and hours. Very few had television. And then we used to play in the middle of the road because there weren't any cars – there were about two cars in the village. And we used to play Hopscotch and Jacks and Five Stones all in the road – because there was nothing to stop us. If anybody was coming, it would be on a pushbike.

Rosie Franklin (Chalford)

Ayurke!

We used to all play together and my mother had a big rocking horse when we were small and we used to all have turns with that. We did play 'Ayurke' all up round the Rack Hill: some would be down in the valley and the rest of them would run up all round the Rack Hill and we would go 'Ayurke!' and they had to tell us where they were. We used to picnic in the woods or up in the fields by the station.

Irene Mayo (Chalford)

More childhood games

We used to play the usual games like 'Ayurke'. Then there was 'Cannon', where you crossed six sticks on a tin and you knocked them off with a ball and then you had to go put them back on. While you was doing this the 'guardian' of the tin would pick up the ball and throw it at you. Then there was what we called 'Salad me Egg': one fella would stand up with his back to the wall as 'buffer' and the other kid would bend down and the other behind him and the rest of them would come and jump on his back. I think it was meant to be called 'Saddle My Hag'. In the summer the meeting place was just on the road (not on the playing field, that was a dump along there), just where the bridge is. If it was

raining we'd go under the bridge, and in the winter we used to meet up by the letter box at the top of Tanner's Pitch because there was a light from the shop there. The shop was Baughan's – it sold mostly sweets, but you could buy tie pins, cotton and tins of milk. Ideal, stuff like that.

Norman Rogers (Chalford)

A penny a dozen

We amused ourselves in ways that have long since gone out of fashion. For instance, we ran for miles bowling an iron hoop with a stick, trying not to let it fall over – not an easy task on an uneven road. It seems, perhaps, rather mindless, but it kept us healthy and out of mischief. When we weren't chasing a hoop, we were chasing each other in a game called 'Hare and Hounds': one group of us chased another group all through the woods and around the fields, after having given them a start and a chance to get away. On rainy days, or days when we couldn't go outside, we played a game similar to bowls but on a smaller scale with coloured glass marbles. The aim was to win the opponent's marbles or the right to swap marbles so that one could boast the most attractive collection. Marbles were popular with us since they cost only a penny a dozen, and baked clay ones were even cheaper: I still have one to this day. That must be classed as the height of sentimentality, as there is nothing of beauty about it!

George Gleed (Brownshill)

Creating a new playing field

We lived right out of the village down at Ashmeads; we had the run of the woods. Out in front of where we lived was actually a hay meadow. The River Frome winds through the middle of that meadow, but you can't see it

Michael Mills' grandparents and family outside Ashmeads Mill, Chalford, in around 1909. From left to right, back row: Philip, Sarah, Charlie and Flora Mills. Front row: Edith, Charles Senior, George, Fanny and Arthur Mills (Michael's father).

now because it's all silted up. The Frome is the little stream that runs by the side of the road. The 'big brook', as we always called it, was a man-made brook for the factories, to take water to the mills.

The Chalford Valley playing field was always a rubbish tip. Believe it or not, they put swings on there even when it was an active rubbish tip in 1938. It was still a tip up until after the war. It was at a much lower level than what it is now, and, after the war, my wife and my parents and all the others got together and formed a committee and they used to hold grand fêtes and all sorts of things to raise money to build that playing field and they had it all levelled out, topsoil put on and the swings put on asphalt. When we was kids

we got bottles off the tip and we would play bombers – the whole place was littered with broken glass. I don't know how we survived!

Michael Mills (Chalford)

Walking up the hill together

I went to school at Chalford Hill and I hated it. I hated it from the minute I started. One of the schoolmistresses was Mrs Mills, Michael Mills' mother; she would come along and collect the two Clark girls – Ev Clark's girls who lived along Ashmeads – then they'd call for me. Then there'd be the girl next door, Janet Bishop, and we used to walk up the hill all together. Mrs Mills by then had really

Above: *Michael Mills in 2003. (Photograph by Peta Bunbury)*

Left: *Michael Mills' mother, Gwen Mills (née Pearce) on her graduation as a teacher from Bristol University in around 1921.*

bad hips and knees and she used to struggle up the hill.

Rosie Franklin (Chalford)

Chalford Hill School

I grew up in Station View – a lot of my friends went to the bottom school but I came up to the top school. Mrs Mills was the teacher there then; she was quite strict. Her son Michael was there then too; he was sometimes in our class. He was a bit older than me, but she would shout at him the same as everybody else. She used to walk from Ashmeads every day. She had bad legs, but she went every day up Coppice Hill to the school and back.

I don't remember much about Chalford Hill School, except that the teacher was Mrs Crook and when my brother started school he hated it and we could not work out why. Our mother took him to Dr Middleton, who told him to get back to school. But the reason was Mrs Crook: she was a lovely old soul, but she had a loud voice and she was one of those who made a lot of saliva when she talked and that was what was frightening him. So they changed him to Miss Ollerenshaw's class and he never looked back, he loved it! I was in Miss Mallet's class – Zena Mallet. Zena and her husband ran the village shop after the war, they ran the Eastcombe shop first. She came from Stroud; her father was the local barber.

Graham Mayo (Chalford)

The teachers at Chalford Hill School in around 1957/58. From left to right, back row: Miss Ethel Crook, Mrs Gwen Mills. Front row: Edris Carter, Mr Morgan, Zena Mallet.

My beautiful hair

I had this really long hair, I could sit on it. My mother wouldn't cut it – she thought it was beautiful and everybody would comment on my hair, my ringlets. I used to have to sit every morning on the chair – at night I'd have it put in rags and in the morning my mother would curl it round her fingers and put in these two huge bows. Mrs Mills'd be outside saying, 'Cooee! cooee!' and my mother would say, 'I'm just tying the last bow'.

Rosie Franklin (Chalford)

Soaking his feet

I was living in Station View with my mother and father and grandfather, Harry Grimmett, the signalman. (My father was a Pearl Insurance agent – all mouth and bicycle clips, as they used to say!) Harry was a nice grandfather, but a very moody man: he would sometimes go two weeks and not speak to anyone. Then, all of a sudden, he would go out one night and he would come in as nice as nine pence. But he had a thing about feet: when we was kids and we'd have our bath in

23

May Queen at Bussage School in around 1957/8. From left to right: John West, Kathy Watkins (née West) Eric Nobes, Judith Davies, Susan Chalk (May Queen), Anita Beavis, Susan Ball, David Bedwell.

front of the fire, one side'd get red hot and the other side'd be cold. He'd say, 'Don't throw that water away, I'll put my feet in there for an hour,' and he used to sit there reading his paper, with his feet soaking. Rain water, mind. Beautiful. Lovely and soft. If ever he thought we wanted a pair of shoes, he was very generous. 'They can't walk about in what they've got, we'll get them a new pair of shoes,' he'd say.

Graham Mayo (Chalford)

Fun and games at school

We used to have a whale of a time at Bussage School: we used to do a lot of plays and go down the church a lot; we used to know how and when to ring the bell; we used to know everything about religion. We did country dancing and things like that. Miss Parker was our headmistress. When we went up to the Manor School, we were all in the bottom form because we hadn't learnt anything at primary school – but we all came top in religious instruction! All the kids from Stroud knew about the Romans, but we didn't have a clue! It took us a couple of years to catch up.

We used to walk all the way to Bussage School from Brownshill. I can more or less remember my first day. My mother walked us there down the steps, very gingerly, hanging on for dear life, and round the back of the school. There was this very cold passage where you hung your coat and you went in the infants class. I can remember playing with sticks in the sand, assembly in the big room (there were only two rooms – the infant room

Above: *Kathy Watkins (née West) standing centre front in around 1960 in a Bussage School play. Her twin brother, John, stands far right.* Below right: *David Collins in the garden at Fir Tree Cottage, Bussage, in around 1934.*

and the big room). There was like a wooden pulpit that the teacher sat on and overlooked everybody. The toilets had this automatic flush system and you were absolutely frightened to death that you'd be in there when it went off. And there was a field round there where you had to be very careful, because in the summer the snakes used to come over and once or twice there were adders and grass snakes in the toilet! And I can remember there was a bit of stone on the wall which was like a horse's saddle, and you could straddle this stone and pretend you were riding horses. And there used to be a hawthorn tree with berries by the wall.

Kathy Watkins (Brownshill)

Mushrooms and skylarks

I spent all my childhood at Fir Tree Cottage in Bussage. Bussage was then just on the western slopes of the hill, nothing above at all. From what is now the recreation ground and across the fields of what is now the Manor Farm Estate to Eastcombe there were no houses at

A photograph showing the Craft School at Brimscombe in around 1912/13.

all. It was our favourite mushrooming spot; there were some old allotments on one side which were still used to some extent. It was a playground for the kids – we could play football as it was mostly grassland. It was full of skylarks. Mushrooms and skylarks were the two things that I remember most of all.

My childhood was a pleasant time – I know my parents weren't well off, but it wasn't apparent. We used to have some wonderful games, we used to have gangs, and build our camps down in the woods below; we used to have bow and arrow competitions, it was a totally different life to what it is now for children. No danger, or conception of danger – just a very free lifestyle.

David Collins (Bussage)

Talented woodworker

I stayed at school till I was thirteen years and ten months. At the Craft school there was woodwork, metalwork, art and science – I could be top in those, no trouble. Then you come to English and Maths and it was a waste of time for me to be honest – I was one of those people who could do most things if I was interested, but algebra and geometry, I couldn't see any point.

The school woodwork master, who lived at the house at Abnash Cross, knew I was very good at woodwork. There was a Captain Disney who lived in a house in Bussage and he'd started up a woodwork business along the bottom and between the two of them, they got me out of school before I was fourteen.

Brian Beavis (Bussage)

Nibbs and George

We had Nibbs and George who did all the work – they were our carthorses. I can remember coming back with them from France Lynch with a load of loose hay, riding on the hayrick. When we got a tractor I was absolutely terrified of it and the noise it made, because we didn't have anything motorized.

Kathy Watkins (Brownshill)

Above: *Bussage in around 1918. Brian Beavis is the child sitting with the lady in the hat, next to the bride, at the marriage of his aunt to Bob Barnfield.*

Right: *Kathy Watkins as a teenager on the tractor at Firwood Farm in around 1967/8.*

Helping mother

We all got up one after the other and we all got washed one after the other in the little back kitchen that we had. We had to go down the garden for the toilet and the washhouse was also down the garden. When Mother was doing the washing, we used to have to stay away from school to look after the other children while she was down in the washhouse. I always remember, when we did go to school, we would come home to dinner and then we always had to take the baby up the road in the pram and get it to sleep before we went back to school. Many the time I went on up the road holding the baby's eyes to make it go to sleep.

Mother used to cook us all meals. We always had a good cooked dinner. That was one thing about my father – he always kept plenty of vegetables in the garden. He had an allotment in the garden and we always had plenty of vegetables. He used to go out shooting rabbits. We lived on rabbits. Mum used to make cakes but she had to be careful – we had an old-fashioned kitchen range and she had to keep turning it round so it didn't get burnt.

Phyllis Smith (Bisley)

One lovely teacher, one tartar!

Being in the infants, we used to have pieces of leather with holes in and we used to have to learn to lace them up. We knit reins too, just knitting really long bits with holes for people's arms to go through. I used to like sewing as I got further up – petticoats and nightdresses and things like that.

We had one teacher called Miss Webb – we used to call her Cobby Web – and Miss Evans, who was lovely. Miss Nation, she was tartar: she used to rap you across the fingers with a ruler! Class one and two and intermediates. Terrible!

Hilda Ruther (Bisley)

Cycling to the High School

Miss Nation was terrible: very, very strict. There was one poor boy whose nose used to run all day and she used to make him sit away from the rest of the class. I felt sorry for him; he wasn't very bright, I don't think. If you talked in class, you had to stand in the corner with your hands behind your back. It was much more disciplined then.

I went on to the High School in Stroud, there were several of us that year. Everybody passed: some went to the Central School and some to the Marling, and we went to High School, me and Joan Magor, the schoolmaster's daughter.

We had to bike there because there wasn't a bus before ten o'clock in the morning. Because my granny and that weren't well off they provided me with a bike from Gloucester. It came towards the end of August and I didn't know how to ride it, so, along by the cemetery in Bisley, a friend lent me her bike to learn. On my first day going to the High School, I went straight over the top of the handlebars and knocked my knee! Nothing very terrible, but that was my start off!

We used to have to wear these horrible hats and, if anybody caught you without one on, you had to go to the headmistress the next day. They were black velour in the winter, with an elastic under your chin and a green and navy band, and in the summer you took the band off and put it round a straw boater. The uniform was navy blue, fleecy-lined knickers and a navy blue gymslip and green and white blouses. In the summer we had blue or green cotton dresses with a white collar and white band round the sleeves. They were still very strict at the secondary schools.

When I was at the High School there were a lot of things that my granny couldn't afford. We used to have to buy our own tennis racquets and hockey sticks and it was all a proper worry, in a way. So, the day I left

Muriel Hunt, seated centre front, on the steps of the Stroud High School, in around 1935

school, I never felt any inclination to go back and be a member of the old girls or anything. I was just glad to leave – I don't know if it was the pressure of having no money.

Muriel Hunt (Bisley)

Stealing the crumbs

Food was scarce, but we were a little bit more fortunate than some. For instance, there was a family who lived on Chalford Hill who were desperate for food. We had a mountain ash tree at the end of the garden with some big flagstones on, and on Sundays we always had a tablecloth on the table for tea and consequently there were always crumbs. I have seen my mother take the tablecloth out to the end of the garden and put the crumbs on the flagstones for the birds, but I've also seen little hands – actually seen hands! – come up and pick the crumbs up. That was the situation then. There was a terrific amount of unemployment. Even in the late 1920s the Button Mill had gradually ceased production of walking sticks, umbrellas, file handles and everything else like that.

I was at school at Chalford Hill School, three minutes from the Rack Hill. I wasn't too bad at school – I did show off once, though, and then I had to go into the toilet and have my mouth washed out with Lifebuoy. I was told I should say jam and butter – not damn and bugger!

Michael Tanner (Chalford)

Michael Tanner and his brother Jim in around 1928. Michael is wearing clothes knitted for him by his mother.

A poor quality photograph of Mr White's top class at Eastcombe School in 1924. From left to right, back row: Cyril Catchet (a 'Home' boy), Eddie Flight, Royston Nobbs, Raymond Vale, -?-. Middle row: Mr White, Nora Davis, Grace Winstone, Ronald Gardiner, George Dutton, Reg Fawkes, John Freebury, Eileen King, Elsie Farmer, Emily Hills (a 'Home' girl, sent to live in Australia). Front row: Vera White, Cissy Davis, Ethel Gardiner, ? May, Theo Armor, Marion Mills, Dorothy Arnold.

The schoolmaster's daughter

Mr White was the headmaster at Eastcombe School; he lived at Chalford. He used to come over with his two eldest daughters, one in the sidecar on the motorbike and one on the back. One daughter, Vera, was a case! She used to go out in the rain and get little frogs and put them in the pencil box, and presently there was such a commotion, everybody was seeing them jumping about. Her father gave her a good telling off. Mr White's sister also taught there. It was a small school in the same building as it is today.

Grace Winstone (Eastcombe)

Heating up the copper

I can remember the gas being brought into Bussage. We had no running water: we fetched our water from a well down in the cellar. Mother didn't have a washing machine, she had a boiler, or copper, down in the kitchen and she had to light a fire underneath it. She used to go down, fetch about eighteen buckets of water from the well, bring it up the steps, get the boiler going, get the washing and then she would have to swill it all and take all the water in buckets up a flight of steps and throw it on the garden. Bath nights, once a week, it was a tin bath in front of the fire and again, the water was brought up from the well, heated in the boiler and then tipped in the bath and that had to be taken up the garden afterwards too.

Pam Clissold (Bussage)

Before Manor Farm

Before the Manor Farm Estate, it was all just open fields up there – we used to walk

Schoolboys on Rack Hill, Chalford, in 1934. From left to right: Jim Tanner, David Young, Michael Tanner, David Wiltshire (a cousin of the Tanners who came to Chalford as an evacuee during the war)

through there. Beautiful wildlife, birds and all sorts. The first building started in the 1950s and it just grew and grew.

Graham Mayo (Chalford)

An outdoor childhood

Before the development at Manor Farm it was all fields up here. There was a big allotments for Bussage and there were pathways we used to get to Eastcombe. For years beforehand, we knew something was going on but it would never happen. They started the new road and then they stopped. There was even a tennis court up there on a flat piece right in the middle of all these fields. My father took us out as children for long walks at weekends, from Frithwood all the way across to Eastcombe and Bisley and back down through. It wasn't for half an hour – these

were really long walks, and once a year we used to walk to Painswick. It was very much an outdoor childhood.

Pam Clissold (Bussage)

The street was our playground

We could always use the street as a playground because there was no traffic, only a horse and cart that used to come to the Co-op in the middle of the street once a day, to bring up bread and groceries I suppose. We used to have big hoops with a thing attached on the hoop to wheel it and we used to do skipping with the two ropes – that was mostly in the playground. There were also whip tops, a stick with a string on, and marbles. We used to get filthy dirty in the school playground digging the holes for the marbles to roll into.

Muriel Hunt (Bisley)

Muriel Hunt as a girl with friends Celia and Peter Stevens on the beach at Weston in around 1930.

Mealtime treat

Mrs Skirton lived next door to us; she was like a second mother to us. If Mum couldn't get back from Stroud at dinnertimes, we had to go in there and then go back to school. Mrs Skirton had a big stone jar just inside her cupboard door, which was full of dried fruit, apricots and pears in syrup. We used to like it, when we went in there, because that was their pudding for after a meal.

Grace Winstone (Eastcombe)

In bed with measles

We didn't have any holidays so we used to think it was wonderful if we got a day at the seaside – it was either to Weston or Barry – but the year they went to Barry I had measles and had to stay in bed for three weeks. But

they brought me back a nice ball, green one side and red the other. Mrs Salmon and Mrs Millen used to run whist drives to raise the money to take the children to the seaside.

Muriel Hunt (Bisley)

Three months in hospital

When one got the measles, the rest of them did. We all had chicken pox together; we used to have to keep away from all the children in the village and go up the road and play. And we all got diphtheria. I was twelve and I was the last to have it. Mother never had the doctor to the rest of them, because they weren't too bad, but I was so ill she sent for the doctor and I was sent to Cashes Green and I was there for three months. I was really very ill. I always remember being in a steam tent for a week. It was like a terrible throat

Rack Hill in around 1932. Norah Tanner, Michael's mother, is with Frankie Gardiner, the bread delivery boy, and his donkey. (Photograph courtesy of Peckham's, Stroud)

infection, you had a job to breathe or eat or speak or anything. I always remember one little girl dying while we were there. There were four or five of us in the ward at Cashes Green with it. It was very catching and we were isolated there. I only saw my mother occasionally because there weren't many buses. I think she used to try and come on a Thursday. I was sad, but there were other children to play with in the wards, so it sort of took it off a bit.

Phyllis Smith (Bisley)

A ha'penny treat

There used to be a Red and White bus service which ran from The Grove at Chalford along Ashmeads to Bakers Mill. When I was a boy, it was one of my treats to pay the ha'penny fare and ride on that bus. I used to run along the towpath to get to Bakers Mill and catch it back to The Grove. People would come down from Oakridge to pick it up to get to Chalford station. The buses used to run every fifteen minutes. There were four drivers who worked on the bus – Fred Stanton (who was married

Michael Tanner in 2003.
(Photograph by Peta Bunbury)

to Mildred Grimmett, Renee's sister), Freddie Bennett, who lived in Rodborough, Hubert King and Frank Washbourne. It was a nice little bus but it stopped running in December 1933.

Michael Tanner (Chalford)

3 A Bustling High Street
and Serving the Hilltop Communities

The whistling butcher

There was a chap up on the High Street, Mr Brown, where you could buy a rabbit; you'd go up and watch him skin it for threepence extra and that made a good dinner. We had rabbit roasted and stewed; I like a rabbit pie, myself. He also sold faggots. Then there was Mrs Mumford, who kept the sweet shop. She had half the door open and you could put your hand over and ask for a pennyworth of sweets, (if you had a penny). Opposite Station View there's the Seventh Day Adventist chapel, which used to be a bakehouse. Fred Smart had the shop opposite the Chalford post office and we used to laugh because, up the hill, by the Plymouth Brethren chapel, was a slaughter house. It's called Sister Mary's Cottage now, and they cut their bacon and all that up there. When you went into the shop and asked for half a pound of bacon, or whatever, Jim Smart would come out with a steel and a knife and he would sharpen it all the way up the hill, to cut you off a bit of bacon. And he'd no sooner come back than somebody else'd come in for something and up he'd go again, with his knife, all the way up the hill – whistling! These Smarts also owned the shop at the bottom of Coppice Hill. I used to help get the bread out of there when they went for dinner.

Irene Mayo (Chalford)

Every kind of shop

Where Noah's Ark is now on the bottom road was the old Pike House. It was originally Gilbey's, then it became Holmes's Stores and they also ran the post office up on Chalford Hill. There was the Co-op down there too, where Mixed Monkey is now, which was big. We used to get all our groceries there. I even remember Mum's number: 1643 and Gran's was 990. It was the number one branch of the Stroud Co-operative Society, as opposed to the Cainscross and Stonehouse Co-operative Society. There was a man named Bingle worked there, and a Miss Philpotts, who came from Stroud way, and Ev Clark, who lived at Ashmeads. There was a bakery there too and old Mr Hemming, the baker, used to go round with a horse and cart and, later, with a van that looked like Corporal Jones' van in Dad's Army! You could send your order in and they would deliver it.

Along the Chalford High Street you had the post office where it still is now and opposite that was Fred Smart's shop. There used to be a little shop attached to the Bell Inn, where Mr Brown used to sell game poultry and that sort of thing. He used to buy rabbit skins by the thousand – they were all hanging up there. The skins went to London and the fur went to make felt hats. I can remember seeing them hanging up down below; there was a sort of porch thing down underneath, and they were all hanging up on

Chalford Central Stores on the High Street, Chalford, c. 1920, also showing the post office on the left-hand side, where it still is today. Smart's Stores boasts 'Noted House for Home Cured Hams and Bacon' above it's shop front. The man walking up the High Street towards the shop is signalman Harry Grimmett, father of Irene Mayo.

W. and A. Gilbey's Stores (seen here around 1900), which became Mann's at the bottom of Old Neighbourhood, is very recognisable as the bike shop Noah's Ark today.

A good view of the Co-op looking down Cowcombe Hill, c. 1960; Halliday's Mill is on the right.

The Bell Inn on Chalford High Street, c. 1930. Mr Brown, landlord and game dealer, is one of the men in the picture.

This extraordinary photograph shows the house built on what is now the car park for the New Red Lion on Chalford High Street, c. 1890. It is indeed a large house and set at a distinctly lower level than the road. The buildings opposite, to the left of the small bakehouse, are long gone, leaving only huge stone arches in the high walls.

strings. He was a licensed game dealer, and he used to sell things like goose eggs, pheasant, partridge, that sort of thing. Brown, father and daughter ran the Bell Inn, then, I remember; the two Miss Browns ran it until it shut down.

Then you had the New Red Lion as opposed to the Old Red Lion. There was a butcher's shop in the buildings that were all pulled down and there was a great big house where the pub car park is now. It was derelict all through the war and we used to play in it. A family named Pegler lived there and Lionel Padin's family lived in it at one time. Then you had the bakehouse opposite, which became the Seventh Day Adventist chapel in 1952.

Just along was the Old Red Lion and, in the house opposite, there was a branch of the Midland Bank. Then you had Miss Gardiner's shop along there: you can still see the shop front. Several people bought it after the Gardiners, but they never made a go of it. It closed in the sixties. Then, just up past there was another pub, the Anchor. It's called Anchor House now, and up till the outbreak of war, Cecil Dean had a little shop there selling greengroceries and cakes and things, which he used to take in a van all round the villages. And on the corner you had Baughan's shop. Just up from there, up Coppice Hill, there was Charlie Wood the baker on the left.

Michael Mills (Chalford)

39

Bone-workers and cabinet-makers

Where that builder's yard is now on the High Street – what was Seville's Mill – they used to do bone-working there. They used to get animal bones and cut them up for knitting needles and grocery hooks; Webb and Peacey's it was called. One of our gang had to see his sister, who was working in there, that's how I came to go in, otherwise I never would have gone. There was a long workshop and many little, fine tooth-saws cutting up these bones: you could say a dozen saws, I should think. You had a job to look through there, because of the dust, and the people who worked in there came out white. Hallidays Mill, where the canal comes out down by the garage, now that was one of the best cabinet-makers in England, Peter Van der Waals – a Dutchman. We always called him Van der Plonk! In the paper – the *Western Press* I think it was – I saw a piece of furniture for sale, just an ordinary chest of drawers effort, for £2,000! Of course, I used to know some of the workers of his – we used to have fish and chips in Stroud on Saturdays.

Norman Rogers (Chalford)

Just like the *Marie Celeste*

Webb and Peacey's was in Seville's Mill, the last cloth mill in Chalford to actually make cloth, then it became a wood and bone-turning factory. I remember it, because it was derelict during the war and we used to play in it as kids. It was closed down in 1938 and it was almost like the *Marie Celeste*, because all these machines were there, with stuff left in all the belts, all connected up. The steam engine was still there, the water wheel was still there. The chap who bought it, just at the end of the war, made a fortune out of selling bonemeal that was underneath the lathes. It had just lain

there for nearly ten years, and he dug it all out and sold it to Gardiners. Webb and Peacey were the last two men to run it as a bone-worker's. They were both Chalford people.

Grandad was originally a bone-turner, he used to turn crochet hooks out of bone for a ha'penny a gross, piecework. He worked at Critchley at Brimscombe. It was all hand-turning; you just had a shaped piece that you turned against the bone. Imagine turning a hundred and forty four of those out for a ha'penny!

Michael Mills (Chalford)

Gum-itchy cheese

There were various shops: a small confectioner's by the village green in Bussage and the two other main shops were both in Brownshill – Mrs Underwood and Mr Marshall. Mrs Underwood's shop was in a wooden shed at the bottom of her garden, she used to have barrels of broken biscuits and the most wonderful cheese, real gum-itchy cheese. That was a regular trip along there.

Dave Collins (Bussage)

'What was it you wanted?'

Sometimes my grandparents would give me a penny and I would rush straight to Lisa Damsell's shop (Lisa was also called Lilla by some people), and buy sweets. Gran told me that when she was a little girl, she also went to the same shop, which was even then served by Lisa – she would buy a farthing's worth of sweets and have three farthings change. Lisa was a tiny lady, just like a doll, and always greeted her customers in the same way, saying, 'What was it you wanted?' Why she always used the past tense puzzled me. Another puzzling invention of hers was the slot in the counter so that she could drop coins through

A pre-Second World War photograph showing the valley end of Chalford High Street and Seville's Mill with the millpond behind, adjoining the canal path and beneath the railway. Seville's Mill was demolished in 1945.

it into the cash drawer – but she had to open the drawer to give change, so it seemed rather pointless in the long run. The old shop was very damp and the stock was low. I imagine this was done purposely, hoping to sell goods before they were marred by the damp atmosphere. I remember one time buying some gobstoppers which must have been in stock for a long time, because not only were they very sticky, but a couple of good hard sucks and they were gone. The sugar in those days came in large sacks which looked to be like fine hessian. Lisa would weigh out as much as a customer wanted into dark blue bags, which she had a special knack of folding. The sultanas and currants were kept in large

tins and I was so pleased whenever Mother sent me to get sultanas, because I always transferred a few into my trouser pocket for later consumption.

There were two other shops in Brownshill in addition to Lisa's: Marshall's, which was a post office and stores combined at the end of the row of Jubilee Cottages, and Underwood's. This shop was a large shed or wooden building, forming part of the boundary of the owners' garden not far from the top of Blackness Hill. Any would-be customers had to pull on the stiff, looped wire which rang a bell in the house and then Mrs Underwood, or one of the family, walked up the path, opened the back door of the shop

Brownshill post office in around 1910.

and came through to the front door to admit the customer. The bell-pull was situated fairly high to stop small children from playing with the bell, but now and then we balanced on each other's shoulders, rang the bell and bought something if we had any money, or ran for it if we hadn't. Looking back, I can't imagine how Brownshill supported three shops, especially as Bussage had a prestigious Co-op store, which attracted most of the trade mainly because of the dividend.

George Gleed (Brownshill)

Well served

My father-in-law worked in the Co-op for forty-seven years. It was a very good store. It was connected to the main Co-op in Stroud and we used to have the main Co-op baker deliver. We could take our orders up to the Co-op on a Tuesday and they would be delivered, by the baker, on Friday. We had Alfie Phipps' little shop; he was a cobbler who

had been injured in the First World War and he used to walk up Bussage Hill, every day, on his crutches. He also sold paraffin and potatoes. Mr Gleed had a paraffin round too. We had Brownshill post office and shop, run by Mr and Mrs Marshall, then Ken and Rita Gorney. Mr and Mrs Underwood had a shop and post office and we always had the shop up at Eastcombe. We were very well served, and didn't need to go down to the valley for anything, really.

We also had the Pincott's at the Ram Inn at Bussage: Maud Pincott ran the public house, but Mr Pincott ran a farm and he owned quite a lot of land. For example, Ashley Drive in Bussage, that was Mr Pincott's field. He also used to deliver milk; Herbert Munday worked for him. We used to leave our cans with a saucer over the top outside the doors to have the milk delivered every morning. Wilf West delivered round Brownshill, with his horse and cart.

Pam Clissold (Bussage)

The Green at Eastcombe, c. 1910.

He'd bake your cake

There was always the Eastcombe shop on the green and, when we were young, Mrs Caldrey used to live in the big house, opposite the pub – Woodview. We used to love to go into her shop, because she had different things and we could get more for our pennies in there. The shop was called Bond's at first. The post office was the house above, the Anthills kept it – Dora Anthill.

In Bussage there was a good Co-op; we used to go there to shop because it was the best place, and if you wanted it delivered, they used to deliver it. Mr Clissold came round for your order on a Tuesday and he would take your book, for your grocery, and you would get it and pay for the next one when he came. Mr Cyril Hemming delivered it all; he lived down in Bliss Mill Cottages in Chalford, and he also delivered for the Chalford Co-op. We got our bread there too.

There was a bakery in Eastcombe: on a Saturday morning, I used to have to go in to Mrs Skirton and she would make a cake and put it in the tin and I would take it along to the baker and he would bake it and you had to go along, before dinner, to get your cake. At Christmas time, a lot of people used to take their turkeys along there for him to cook.

Grace Winstone (Eastcombe)

Bisley's sweet shop

There was a girl I was friendly with who used to live with her auntie at the sweet shop in Bisley, but she wasn't allowed to have any sweets! She used to have to deliver *The Citizen.* Her auntie was very strict; her name was Hilda Taylor. There was another sweet shop along towards the cemetery – there was a steep pitch up on to the next road and on the corner there was a sweet shop that Miss Burford had, but she didn't get a lot of trade. Then there was Brown's shop – that was the most popular, I think; if you had a ha'penny you used to stay here with your nose pressed

Stroud Road, Bisley, in around 1900-05. Mr and Mrs Brunsdon are carrying pails.

up to the glass to see how much you could get for a ha'penny. You didn't have a ha'penny very often.

Muriel Hunt (Bisley)

Anything from a needle to an elephant

Our corner shop then was on the opposite side to where it is now. There was the Co-op, then there was a draper's shop, Kilminsters, where you could buy anything from a needle to an elephant! She sold practically anything you could think of, it was a wonderful shop. Then there was another grocer's shop, down the bottom of the village. There were three pubs then: there was the Stirrup Cup and the George in what is now the post office, and the Bear Inn.

Phyllis Smith (Bisley)

Hard work at the Valley Inn

On 8 March 1952, Jean and I got married and went to live at the Valley Inn, Chalford. It made life that much easier for her mum and dad because we were that much younger and we worked there, as well. It was hard work. You kept the pub – the pub didn't keep you. Come Wednesday nights, most people would come in and say, 'A pint, Mike, and the change of ten bob, please.' They didn't have any money, but they would have a drink and the change of a ten bob note, then Friday night, they would come in with the ten bob note. They would sub, rather than putting it on the slate.

It was a sixteen-hour day and, because of the attitude and the discipline of Jean's parents, Harry and Elsie Whiting, everything was done the night before; nothing was left untidy. It was something you did without any consideration or thought, it was an automatic thing, you could not come downstairs next

Church Hill, Bisley.

morning and face dirty ashtrays and empty pint mugs. So it resulted in an extra hour's work after closing time: half past ten in the summer and ten o'clock in the winter.

In those days, we were the other side of the river Frome, so consequently we were in Minchinhampton parish; the railway line is the boundary now, but then it was the brook. Consequently, if you went from Chalford to Brimscombe, you went from Chalford where the Valley Inn is now, and the next pub was the Red Lion, which was on the other side of the brook and had a half an hour's difference in opening and shutting times to what we did. So, when it was your turn to shut at ten o'clock, the evacuation went to the Red Lion, later on it was from the Red Lion back up to the Valley, because of the change in the agricultural laws and extension of daylight hours. Then, as you went on down, you had the Company's Arms by the Roundhouse, then you had the Carpenter's on the right-hand side at St Mary's, then you had the

Queen's Head, right on the corner at St Mary's, then the Victoria, The Kings Arms, The Port and The Ship at Brimscombe – they were all geographically situated so that within five minutes of closing time, you could be in another pub!

You'd call time and they would be happy to go, but at half past ten, when they were reluctant, Jean's father would call in a very authoritative manner, 'Drink up please. Time, gentleman.' And they usually went, too. We didn't have any nonsense at all. When we used to get invaded by people from the Duke of York or the King's Head in France Lynch on a Sunday evening, having a stroll round, he'd say 'Come on, you from the hilltops, you mountaineers; it's time you went.' And they would go. They were 'casuals', they weren't what you'd call locals. He served everyone who came into the pub – he'd give a tramp a drink, but he'd tell him he didn't want to see him anymore. He would give them a bit of bread and cheese; there

A view of the Railway Tavern, Brownshill, as it was during the last century. Although situated high above Brimscombe station, it was opposite the footpath leading down the hill to the main road and the station, hence its name.

were quite a few about in those days. Jesse Miller, for instance, was one who lived along Ashmeads.

Michael Tanner (Chalford)

A real old pub

In Brownshill, opposite the Hermitage Cottage where we used to live, there was a pub called the Railway Tavern – it was a real old pub. We could not believe it when we first went in there: we sat in what looked like a front room – it had no bar in it at all. You placed your order with a landlady, who was usually wearing a hat and coat because it was so cold and walking about with a tin tray. She had to go into a room in the back where all the beers were in barrels and she'd draw it from a tap. There were cinema seats in rows –

that was where you sat. Some of the chaps there were really broad.

David Collins (Bussage)

People walking everywhere

A lot of people from Chalford worked in the mills. Of a morning, you'd see all the people from Oakridge, Frampton Mansell coming along and they all used to sort of 'gather' people. My dad's mate used to come down from Oakridge and he used to go 'Oi, Stan' and then our dad'd go out with his case and off they'd walk along together, and that's how it was. The buses were chock-a-block – they used to go every twenty minutes (every ten on a Saturday) and they were always full and always double-deckers. It was the same at night. Coming down the hill, down Marle

Rosie Franklin in 2003. (Photograph by Peta Bunbury)

Hill especially, people'd be running down there of a morning to catch that bus, and back up at night – people never thought anything of it.

Rosie Franklin (Chalford)

Life down at Belvedere

St Mary's had hooters, all the mills did, to give you five minutes' warning to get there on time. St Mary's made sticks at that time: walking sticks, umbrella handles, all sorts. They make them from a sort of withy, a supple branch grown near the brook. All through Belvedere there were withy trees. My father was a blacksmith; he operated from Belvedere where all those houses are now; that was all our ground at one time. He was a good blacksmith; he learnt his trade there and went on working there. He owned it, eventually. The horse was the mainstay at one time. You had to measure the horse's foot in those days and make the perfect shoe. I've sat and watched him make many a horseshoe. There was a forge and an anvil, and a fire going with great, big bellows. It was a vertical bellows; the arm was at the side. My father got tired of his work. The horses weren't like the ponies are today: they were great, big, heavy things with feathers on their feet. They had to be washed off because it was awful to shoe a horse with dirty feet. It was the mud, you see: there was no tarmac then. We had boots and it was only horse tracks we walked in – muddy in the winter and dusty in the summer. They didn't have metal roads until I was a biggish girl, I think, because we used to have to clean our shoes every day.

Mabel Smith (Chalford)

47

4 To Your Door
Delivering the Goods

George Gleed Snr's oil round

My grandfather was a skilled engineer, but the wages were so low that he gave it up and bought a horse named Tramp and a cart, and started a paraffin round, or 'oil round' as it was more popularly known. He began this business in the 1920s and was soon making a good profit. He then sold Tramp and bought a younger horse named Dolly. By 1937 he felt that he had enough to live on, because there was no inflation in those days, and he could just cultivate his garden and perform odd jobs for some of the farmers and villagers. When I came home from school one afternoon, Dad was really excited: 'Gramp has given me the oil round!'. I felt so happy for him. Father built up the round even more, and the profits gave him about three times the average wage. With one of my sisters working as well, we were on the crest of the wave at last. There were no more patches on my trousers and no more handed-down clothes from my cousins. We had a full larder and full bellies – what bliss!

George Gleed (Brownshill)

The Crews of Pontings Farm

My husband's parents, Nora and Albert Crew, went to live at Pontings Farm, France Lynch as newly-weds in 1930, Albert having served in the army throughout the First World War, mostly in France. In those days, Pontings Farm was a small dairy farm, consisting of approximately forty acres. The milk was taken daily, in churns, by horse and trap to Chalford station where it was put on a train for London.

Nora and Albert had two sons: Bert Junior and my husband, Norman. Farming was very depressed and many farmers had difficulty making a living, so, in 1936 the opportunity arose to buy a milk round in Chalford Valley. This continued until after the Second World War when the milk round was extended, taking in a large part of France Lynch. A Lister engine provided electricity and lighting; a large Rayburn provided all hot water for dairy and household. The cows were milked very early, then the milk was cooled and bottled ready for delivery. Eggs and cream were also delivered. Norman took over the business and milk was delivered not by horse and cart anymore, but by Land Rover, seven days a week, assisted by Bert and others.

Yvonne Crew (Waterlane)

Harry on the bread round

I went to Chalford Hill School – it was the only school I went to and I went there until I was fourteen. With it being wartime, we did lessons in the morning and went potato picking in the afternoons – we did field work. Then I went on the bread round. I worked for Miss Florence Workman of Workman's Bakery, France Lynch. The Point Cottage, on the corner of Brantwood Road and Dr

George Gleed and his father on the 'oil round', c. 1935.

Pontings Farm before it was demolished and rebuilt facing the other way.

France Lynch, c. 1930.

Middleton's Road, used to be a bakery. Where the five new houses are along there and the new vicarage, all that was our bakery. We used to have pigs out in the paddocks and we had meal sheds. We delivered bread and meal out for chickens; people used to have bags of meal to mix in with their potatoes.

Florence, Dennis and Raymond Workman used to run the bakery. I used to go out delivering with Dennis. Raymond used to do all the baking and he had a chap who lived at Bisley who used to come and help him make the bread. They used to start at nine at night and work through, so you had fresh bread to deliver when you went out in the mornings. Fridays, they used to come in at six — I used to help in the bakehouse as well, when they were short.

We used to do deliveries to all of France Lynch, Chalford and the High Street; we used to go as far as The Bourne, then up the Toadsmoor Valley, Eastcombe, Bussage and Brownshill and then up as far as Camp, and we used to branch off to Calfway and come out the other side of Bisley. We used to get winters then, and you couldn't take the van down through. We used to go across two fields and down round to a Mr Sunny Young — just for one house, we used to do nearly a mile there and back to where you started!

Harry Cadwallader (Chalford)

Putting in the sewer

My father, George Jackson, bought the milk round off Sidney Tuck, a farming family from Frampton Mansell; they produced the milk and sold it. My father had come down here from Yorkshire on holiday, to stay with his brother and he liked it round here so much that he decided to come and live here, and brought us all, lock, stock and barrel.

I remember that the sewer came here when we were doing the milk round in the late 1950s. Of course, everybody had septic tanks

The sewer being put through Chalford Valley in around 1960.

until then. I remember that more than Harry, because I delivered milk to all the houses you can see along the Rack Hill as you're driving up Cowcombe Hill. My father'd drive along Chalford Valley and do all the right-hand side and I'd get out of the van and walk up the lanes and down the lanes. Of course, they were only footpaths, and they were digging them out completely. There were mostly Irish navvies doing it and they were lovely. Because it were wet and muddy and slippery and I couldn't walk, they used to pass my hand-crate along, all the way up, and they used to come back and pick me up and carry me along where they'd dug it out. They brought the sewer up through the Barley Grounds from Dimmelsdale to just below the vicarage at France Lynch.

Muriel Cadwallader (Chalford)

Taking over the milk round

When Muriel's father retired I took the milk round over. We had no intention of doing it; I was a builder at the time. Mind, we always helped with the milk round, we always had to. That's the trouble with being family: my father–in–law only lived in the cottages at the back, so we was too near to dodge it!

Harry Cadwallader (Chalford)

We were just talking about the milk round and my dad retiring, and I said, 'Would you like it?' and Harry said, 'Yes, I think I would.' I said, 'Well, you get up there quick and tell him we'll have it'. But he'd already sold it to Stroud Creamery and we didn't know. So then, we franchised it back and just

Harry Cadwallader on the milk round.

took enough for us to do: the Hill part and France Lynch. My father had had too much, he'd a lot of help. He used to go along the High Street, to Frampton Mansell, Sapperton and Aston Down. All the other milk rounds kept retiring and my father kept buying them out: Duncan Young, Norman Crew and Fred Halliday.

Muriel Cadwallader (Chalford)

Peat off the back of a lorry

There were other bakeries in the valley. There was Mr Wood down Coppice Hill and Mr Smith down in the valley, so I don't know how we acquired all those customers in the valley. Most of ours started at the top, then it sort of progressed to Eastcombe, Bussage, Brownshill, Bisley, Oakridge (even Far Oakridge), Waterlane and Tunley.

It was awful driving round in the winter. I shall never forget one Friday afternoon; it was teeming with rain and I was wet through and still had to do Bourne's Green and Oakridge and all the rest. I got towards Smart's Farm at Bourne's Green where there was a nasty bend. A lorry and I met and we only just pulled up in time; we both got out and said what we thought of each other! We commiserated with each other about the weather and I said, 'Whatever's that you've got on your lorry?' and he said it was peat. I said, 'That's interesting!' We could get very little fuel. So he said, 'Oh yes, I'm taking it round to Mr Peacey,' who was the butcher. So I said, 'Well, will you be getting any more?' So he said that he thought he probably would. So I said, 'Well, when you go to Mr Peacey, you'll be passing where I live. Could you go in and ask my mother if she would like you to get her some?' 'Oh yes, yes', he

Muriel Cadwallader with her father's milk van in 1973. While delivering the milk, they also used to collect old newspapers, which they took to Mr and Mrs Alfred Leeding in Chalford for the WI. The Leedings would recycle the paper and any money made would come back to the village for good causes.

said, 'but I couldn't possibly let her have any of the stuff I've got on the lorry because of Mr Peacey.' Well, it went on getting wetter and wetter and later and later getting home. I got home and I got the wrath of God from my mother! She said 'How dare you? How dare you? Telling that man that I'd buy all that peat! You've cost me £22!' That was an awful lot of money in those days. She said 'When have you ever done what I tell you to!' I said, 'I didn't!' She said, 'He told me you said if he

called on me I would buy it!' I said, 'I didn't! He was going to Mr Peacey!' Anyway, she'd bought it. It had gone down into the cellar. She kept bringing up this business of it costing her £22. But we found that we had an ideal boiler in the kitchen, you see, and we found if we put two pieces of peat in it overnight, when we got up in the morning we had plenty of hot water to have a bath and we hadn't used our precious anthracite. So these two pieces of turf went on every day

Baker Arthur Young of France Lynch with his wife Ellen and two daughters Kathleen (left) and Muriel (Pam Turner's mother) in around 1906.

and even when we left several years later, we still had some peat left over! I used to say, 'Remember the peat, mum?' and we used to have a good laugh! I heard her say to somebody, one day, 'The best thing I ever did is when I bought that load of peat!' and I wasn't too far away and I said 'It was me!' I couldn't help laughing.

Florence Workman (France Lynch)

Two deliveries a day

I can remember seeing Bertie Crew from Pontings Farm with the yoke and pails on. Day Crew had Westley Farm and another brother had a farm at Frampton Mansell. Down at Ashmeads, we used to get milk from Tuck at Frampton Mansell and Stafford who lived in those First World War billets at Aston Down. They delivered milk twice a day then, as nobody had refrigeration, and the morning and evening milk were never mixed.

Michael Mills (Chalford)

The bakery at France Lynch

My mother and I came to live with my grandmother when my father died. She had to look after the shop, the bakery in France Lynch, which was built by my great-grandfather. My grandfather took it over when the First World War was on, but they couldn't get anyone to help with the baking, so mother left school to do it. She also took all

Muriel Young (Pam Turner's mother) and her sister Kathleen in around 1906 in the pony and trap used to deliver bread from France Lynch bakery to the outlying villages.

Wilf West, the Brownshill milkman.

the bread out to the surrounding villages in a pony and trap. She wasn't very old either. She used to go to Oakridge quite a bit: that's where she delivered bread – and course, my grandmother came from Oakridge so she knew a lot of people. But one day the horse bolted and left her over there and she said she was so worried, because she knew her mother would be cross with her. But when she got back the horse was already home!

We used to always have a lot of people to stay at Christmas. Once, when it was deep snow, mother's cousin from Weston and his friend came and they said to Mum, 'Oh, you can't take the bread out today' and they decided to go to Oakridge instead of her. They set off – of course, they couldn't take the pony and trap because the snow was too deep – and my grandmother said, 'You be back here for lunch at one o'clock'. Mum said they had to walk the walls because the snow was so bad. Anyway, they didn't come back and my grandmother was getting so cross. Then, Mum heard a noise and she came out in the kitchen and there they were, sitting in the bread baskets, tittering like a couple of schoolboys. They had been and delivered the bread to Oakridge and at that time everybody in Oakridge made homemade wine and everyone had given them a glass!

Pam Turner (France Lynch)

Deliveries to the villagers

I remember the local milkman who lived at Brownshill, Wilf West. He used to come round in a horse and cart, two-wheeled, with the big milk churns inside. He would come down with either a pint or a two–pint pail and pour it into the jugs at the door. He had the brass half-dippers, which hung on the side of the can, and he would scoop it out and measure whatever you wanted that particular day.

I remember the insurance man used to call to collect insurance. I remember bread being delivered. In 1948 when the winter was very, very bad and the village was cut off for many weeks, I was a teenager and I had a big sledge. We put a tea chest on the back of it and myself and a couple of friends went over to the nearest baker's – Workman's in France Lynch – and collected tin loaves and we filled up the tea chest with them and came back and distributed them round the village. We had meat deliveries too, a bit later on, and very reliable vegetable deliveries – Mr Price came round for many years.

David Collins (Bussage)

Delivering to Catswood

I used to take the milk round – we used to have it in cans – and on a Sunday morning I used to go off with all these cans and on my little finger I had a cream can and I had to carry that right down the bottom of the village. It was just a job to do for a shilling a week. I collected the milk from Mr Skinner's farm and the meat from Skinner's too and took it along to Catswood on Saturday afternoons. I used to walk with my butcher's basket on my arm. I only delivered to the one farm – Andrews the name was, Ernie and Jack.

Hilda Ruther (Bisley)

Sid and his ice cream sidecar

Before the war came along to spoil it, weekends in the summer were very enjoyable: one of the reasons was that on Sunday afternoons Sid Moseley the ice cream man came round with his motorbike and sidecar. Sid came from Chalford Hill, his black hair brushed straight back from his forehead, looking very smart. He was a kindly man,

Above: *Sid Moseley, the ice cream man, in around 1935*

Left: *Sid's sidecar.*

Sid later sold his ice creams from a van.

popular with children and adults alike, who he summoned by ringing a handbell. The sidecar had been adapted to become a large chest and when selling the ices the lid was held open with a prop. Inside was a large tub of ice cream, wafers and cornets. The dearest ices were only a few pence and an old ha'penny bought a very small cornet. Sid also came round Brownshill one evening in the week, but for most of us this treat was strictly for weekends only. Sid purchased a van later and a shop, but he sold up and retired, which was quite a loss to Chalford and the district.

George Gleed (Brownshill)

5 The Weekend
Leisure Time and the Church

Sport was my life

Sport was always my life. Football was the only sport on a Saturday – it was the only thing to look forward to. I played for Chalford Hill – we won the Gloucestershire Northern Senior Amateur Cup when we played Stonehouse down on Stroud rugby football ground in 1937.

Norman Rogers (Chalford)

Local sporting heroes

If things had been different, Graham Mayo would have played cricket to a really top level. He was a brilliant county all-rounder. But in those days you needed your own car and he had to rely on public transport. Norman Rogers and Jumper Dean both had trials for England division football: Norman was left back. They were the ultimate in local football – brilliant!

It was a penny for children at The Sycamores and twopence to get in at Brimscombe Meadow. In 1938, an estimated crowd of 1,400 watched Brimscombe and Chalford on Easter Monday.

Michael Tanner (Chalford)

The Chalford Valley Juniors

We had a postman in Chalford called George Walder; he got interested in forming a youth club. We'd always had a little football team that we'd started ourselves called Chalford Valley Juniors. We played occasionally. Walder got to hear about it and his round was Aston Down – Chalford post office had a sub-post office up on the camp at that time. He got friendly with the commanding officer up there, a chap named Clark, and he talked to him and he gave us all the facilities up there. We could go up once a week and use the gymnasium, we could use their field for some matches, we could use their changing room and their showers and we could use their cricket pitch in the summer. He even supplied us with our first set of shirts. Eventually we got into a Stroud Youth League. In the pleasure ground up at Chalford Hill there was a little wooden hut and Walder started a youth club in there. He'd finish work as a postman at about six o'clock in the evening, walk up Cowcombe Hill, have his tea and then go down Marley Lane, up Coppice Hill to the youth club and back down again at night! People wouldn't do that today.

Graham Mayo (Chalford)

Saturday afternoons off

For six months I went to work over on John Cobb's brother's farm. He had an experiment with Jersey cows. I went because he had tractors; it was for one summer from the end of the football season, because I used to play for Bussage. Then, when the football season started again, I said no, I wanted Saturday

Chalford AFC, the 1937 Gloucestershire Northern Senior Amateur Cup winners. From left to right, back row: Frank Fuller, Stan Freeman, Les Pearman, Philip Hill, Norman Rogers, Ron Franklin, Mr Freeman (First Aid). Front row: Ron Goodship, ? Porter, Lewis 'Jumper' Dean (Captain), Harry Gardiner, Bert Cousins.

George Walder the postman, and his Chalford Valley Juniors in 1945/46. From left to right, back row: K. Weaver, Tony Dean, G. Gardiner, G. Walder. Middle row: P. Shields, K. Staddon, G. Dean, J. Smith, Graham Mayo. Front row: P. Baglin, H. Stafford, P. Bingle

afternoons off. Playing for Bussage was more important than working on this farm.

Chalford had a very good team in those days. Bussage team weren't in the Northern Senior League; we were in the top Stroud leagues and, although I had to check every week, I was a permanent player of Bussage first team. But it was my life really, it was that important. Bill Collins used to more or less run the club. He used to make sure the pitch was done and we would have cars here to carry the teams to the away matches. We used to play up here, on the College Ground in Bussage. We never used to play on the Recreation Ground at Bussage because it had to be all flattened. That was right up to the war really.

Brian Beavis (Bussage)

A shock for Gwen!

My husband George used to play for Bisley against Chalford Hill. The Bisley Robins wore red tops and white shorts and they won several cups. He was captain, and I used to wash the shirts. The team used to have their baths up at the Reading Room in Bisley, up the steps. All these bungalow baths used to be there and I used to go and put the boiler on. One day, I was a bit late taking the clean towels along; I went running up the steps and I didn't know the footballers had come down, and I opened the door with these towels and there were all those naked footballers there! Coo! I just threw the towels down and shut the door, quick! There were six bungalow baths – they used to have to take it in turns to get all the mud off.

Gwen Millin (Bisley)

Bisley ladies' cricket team

We had a ladies' cricket team in Bisley and so did Painswick. When we played them, we used to have to cycle over there and play our game and cycle home again. We used to play up Vanderbreen Street. Hill Paul's had a team

The young Brian Beavis in 1946 with two of his early taxis.

Mrs Ruck keeping wicket with Muriel Hunt in the field.

and the Stragglers were an all female team too. A Mrs Ruck used to be the wicketkeeper. You had to have eleven ladies in a team and there must have been more than that and they were all from Bisley. That was our social life.

Muriel Hunt (Bisley)

Nicking wild daffs!

I was very much a country girl – we would just play in that stream for hours in the summer. It never got as low as it is now, never. We could still swim in it, and we used to go up to Mrs Holland's – up to that big house – and we used to nick wild daffs and sell them on the side of the road. There were so many people walking from the mills. Threepence a bunch or something; it'd be about a penny today.

Rosie Franklin (Chalford)

'Wooding' with the family

One of my favourite pastimes in those days was when the whole family went 'wooding' to help keep the home fire burning. This was more difficult than anyone would imagine as the floor of the wood was almost picked clean by other wood gatherers. We used to go along to the College Wood and Father's strong arm was put to good use by throwing a weight tied to the end of a washing line over a dead or dry branch. A sharp tug or two would bring the branch crashing down. I was too young to be of any real help, but I remember carrying home some of the smaller pieces and then we would have a good fire, followed by baked potatoes, hot buttered toast and scalding cups of cocoa.

George Gleed (Brownshill)

A pottery lesson at Westley Farm in around 1975.

An alternative lifestyle

We started our free school – I'd sent Rachel to Wynstones, and then John and Maggie Mills, Popsy and Julian Usborne and us with Matthew and Barney decided we wouldn't send them to school; we'd educate them ourselves in the Valley Inn and at Westley Farm.

It was wonderful because when our kids were small, it was just amazing round here. It was just the best ever. We were all into self-sufficiency: we all had our goats and we had lambs and pigs and chickens and so we'd take it in turns looking after the children. One of us would make the bread, one of us would make the lunch and that's how it was. Our children would sleep out under the stars or they'd make dens up in the woods, down at the park, up on the farm. We'd just light a fire

and they'd just sleep down there and us women would go down and cook on it. They all wandered around with no clothes on – we were known for it. They just did what they wanted. And somebody would look out for them. All our children now are very close; it's formed an amazing bond between us women, which will never be broken.

Rosie Franklin (Chalford)

Car and motorcycle trials

Bussage Hill wasn't even surfaced in those days; it was just a sort of a rough track where they used to have car and motorcycle trials. That was one of the highlights of the village – to go and see the early car and motorcycle trials. There was a stream at the top which

Fishing in Chalford Valley in 1980.

Motocross in 1946. Fifty-two riders from all over the world came to this scramble at Bisley. Brian Beavis came in twelfth on his own bike.

went into a trough for cattle and, whenever we knew there was going to be a trial coming on, we used to go and dam the stream and send the water down Bussage Hill to make it more exciting to watch.

David Collins (Bussage)

The biggest car trial was known as the London to Gloucester. In those days they used to start from London and do all the hills round here. We've got several big hills round here, like the 'W' at Nailsworth and, of course, Bussage Hill, which was rough stones and all that. Baughan from Stroud had a car; he always entered, as did his two secretaries, two girls. They used to drive. There used to be MGs and Singers. You had a man on each hill and it was a matter of just getting up the hill and how far you got up. I had a car called a Jowett; a twin-cylinder, but it had big wheels and it was quite slow. It wasn't a sports car as such. I put my own body on it and made it in the garage, here. Because it was slow, it went 'chug chug'; it never used to spin if the track was muddy. The sports cars would just spin themselves to a standstill, but mine would go up very well.

Brian Beavis (Bussage)

Playing with fire

I remember setting the Cowswell Banks on fire – not on purpose, of course. We would have our campfires down there and, later on in the year, when the fields were covered with bracken and very dry, when they burnt, they burnt and we would run! On the few occasions when Toadsmoor Lake froze, all the lads and practically everyone in the village would go down there and skate. We didn't have skates, of course, but that didn't stop you from trying and sliding – that was quite a regular thing.

David Collins (Bussage)

Skating on the lake

When Toadsmoor Lake was frozen, we used to go down and see it; we wouldn't get on the water. But a fellow we knew from Bisley, he came and he went on the lake and he fell down through the ice! Anyway, they got him to the Woodman's Cottage. (Everybody calls that house along by the lake Keeper's Cottage, but it's not; it's Woodman's Cottage. Keeper's Cottage is the one down in Bismore). Mr McOwen had the one by the lake and we used to go down, because the Lady Dorrington had a couple of peacocks down there, so when we was kids we used to go down and chase the peacocks round. Our neighbours, Mr and Mrs Skirton, used to take us down there for a walk. In the autumn we really loved that because we walked in deep, deep leaves.

Grace Winstone (Eastcombe)

Visiting the family

We got the first van in 1936... I remember the horse and cart before that. There were two horses; one was Tom and the other was Dinah. When things got too much for them, well that's when we got one van and one horse, then two vans and no horses. My father's parents lived at Cowley on the other side of Birdlip and occasionally, on a Sunday afternoon, we went over with pony and trap to see Grandpa John. Then one of my father's brothers lived at Shipton Olive, which is quite a way the other side of Cheltenham and Andoversford and, on rare occasions, we went out to see them, clip-clopping with the horse. Dad used to say, 'It's not fair on the horses, not fair for them to work six days a week and then work on Sunday', so it was rare, but we did go. But we had to get out and walk up Eagle Pitch, the other side of Camp. Mother would ride, but the rest of us, we walked. We always called that house Eagle House: that house with

A postcard showing skaters on Toadsmoor Lake in 1905.

Ice skating on Toadsmoor Lake in 1907/8 showing Woodman's Cottage.

the eagles on top. When we were children, my father told us that when the clock struck twelve, the eagles were going to come down and have their lunch. Denis and I believed it. He told us that, when we were small.

Florence Workman (France Lynch)

Dances in Bisley

I was friendly with Norman's cousin, Audrey Skinner, now Audrey French, who lives in Bisley. We used to go to dances together – a lot of farmers and young farmers dances. They called them balls in those days. We always went to St Patrick's Ball, the Police Ball and the Young Farmers Ball – it was a sort of ritual; you invariably met the same people.

Yvonne Crew (Waterlane)

We had a dance at the Institute every Saturday night when I was a teenager – that was a red letter day! I worked in Woolworths in Stroud and Saturdays used to be really hard work in those days. I used to come home dead tired, but as soon as I'd had a wash and got dressed up, I was ready and raring to go. My mum was the caretaker at the Institute and in the summer, we used to have to go up and shut the windows. My husband – he was my boyfriend in those days – he used to come up with me and we used to practise dancing before we shut the windows, so we were well in.

Gwen Millin (Bisley)

We used to always have whist drives and a dance on a Saturday night and there was a band – that was really something. I didn't get home from work until about nine o'clock on a Saturday night but I made a point of getting washed and changed and ready to go up to the Institute. I would never miss the dance!

Muriel Hunt (Bisley)

The Pompian Dance Band outside the Institute at Bisley in around 1935. From left to right: -?-, Harry Dean (trumpet), Sid Moseley (drums), George Hale (violin), Miss Nation (piano).

Courting – Bisley style

We used to go to church every Sunday night and the teenaged boys always used to go and sit in the back of the church. After church, we all used to go for a walk along the Chalford Road and that's how we picked up with one another. There were two or three girls and we each picked one of our own. We cast up a ha'penny who should have who! I tossed a ha'penny and I got William and I stuck with him. He was my first love and my last. Never had anybody else.

Wednesdays and Sundays, they were the only two days we were allowed out and I always had to be in by ten o'clock. We always used to go walking: used to go miles in the dark, chatting. It was a long time before we were allowed to take them home. I always remember, one night, we were a bit late coming in after ten o'clock because we'd been to Cheltenham to the pictures. When we got in Dad was waiting for us. 'Where have you been to at this time of the night?' he says, 'I suppose you stopped in Cranham Woods?' And Bill looks at him and says, 'If we're going to do anything wrong, we'll do it before ten o'clock, as well as after.' That shut my father up – he never said anything after that. Well it's quite true isn't it? But they both approved of him. We courted for seven years; I was twenty-three when we got married; he was two years older than me.

Phyllis Smith (Bisley)

Joining the Girl Guides

I was a Girl Guide for years – Bisley Guides – and when they packed in, I went over to Eastcombe. I went until I was married. We used to do lots of learning and Red Cross and signalling and things like that and then we use to go away on camp once a year in tents – we had some good times in the Guides.

Phyllis Smith (Bisley)

Bisley could be isolated, but we used to do things with Eastcombe. It was to do with the church really, because the vicar from Bisley used to take the services at Eastcombe Church. If you wanted to join the Guides you had to walk to Eastcombe, which was over two miles of course. My granny wouldn't let me go, and that didn't make me very happy. I used to keep trying, but I was never allowed to go. My granny thought it wasn't suitable.

Muriel Hunt (Bisley)

Dancing at the British Legion

Stan was stationed at Aston Down during the war, so he used to get up to all the dances at the British Legion. That's how most of us met. I met him in 1945, at the end of the war, and we used to have two dances a week at the British Legion. Of course, it was the making of the war for us; there was never anybody around to do anything with. My mother's sister and her son and Derek Matthews had a band and they used to play at the Church Rooms in France Lynch.

Pam Turner (France Lynch)

A ride in a plane

In 1927, when I was sixteen, an aeroplane came up here and landed on the second field, where the Manor Farm Estate is built now. It was one of the first ones – it was open and you could have a ride. Everybody crowded round to have a ride on the aeroplane. I was on the labour at the time and I couldn't afford to go, but Mum found the money. I think it was five shillings a trip. You had to go up, one behind the other and go round and come back. It was an open cockpit and it was cold up there. There was this man from Bussage who used to get up to the pub, and a lot of the men persuaded him to go up in the aeroplane.

Well, he went up, but he was in a shocking state when he come down! He'd been drinking – he was really out. I went up in an aeroplane up at Aston Down, when I worked there, too. There was a head man called Snowy and he used to come from London, and he said, 'Any of you girls want a ride in the aeroplane?' so off we went.

Grace Winstone (Eastcombe)

One bright summer day an aeroplane landed in the Manor Farm fields. Local people were offered flights for ten shillings, but obviously, only a few of the better off people could afford this, as to us, that sum could buy many essential items for the house. The local postmaster went up for a flight and they tell me he had an upset stomach whilst flying, but whether from fear or excitement I never found out. There were very few aeroplanes about at that time, so my whole family went up to see it.

George Gleed (Brownshill)

Ashmeads Fair

Ashmeads Fair didn't happen every year. It happened every two or three years. It took place on the field past what is the playground now. It was a small fair with coconut shies, a greasy pole and a competition with a woman who baked hot puddings, to see who could eat the first one. That used to be a proper field; we used to play cricket and football down there and they used to keep the stream clear and mow it too: there was a hayrick at the far end. But it was always a swampy field with the river running through it, especially in winter.

The Chalford Feast was something else. It was a much bigger affair. At one time it stretched from St Mary's to Chalford station. It used to go on for a few days. I used to chase the girls there, but only when they weren't looking!

Norman Rogers (Chalford)

A very poor quality photograph taken of the de Havilland two-seater plane which took the locals for rides up at Eastcombe.

Ashmeads Fair in 1913. The field on which this event was held is beyond the Valley Playing Field and is now very marshy and houses nothing more than a few beehives. Irene Grimmett (born 1903) is pictured centre front with her sister dressed in a white hat. She remembers the fair being held on that field, the band and the greasy pole – the champion of which was Mr Tubby Franklin, the donkey man!

Chalford Feast

Chalford Feast used to be held in the Belvedere fields. The stalls were right up to the Company's, then right round by the Black Gutter and the river, up into the main road and round the shop. They didn't have to come in until after eight o'clock on a Sunday, the first Sunday after 12 August, that was. There were horses, roundabouts, pony rides, sway boats, shooting galleries, coconut shies, candy floss, greasy poles and all sorts. Mrs Odie Gardener used to have the brandy snap stall. It was a major event. It generally came on a Sunday and lasted a couple of days and then went on to Frampton-on-Severn. The stallholders came from all over Gloucestershire. Most men used to slide along to the Company's after about half an hour though.

Mabel Smith (Chalford)

George Gleed's boy

Sometimes the Boxing Booth would come around to local fairs or shows in those days; it was a golden opportunity for Dad to make a few pounds because there were very few who could stand up to him for very long. He was far better than the over-rated, over-paid imitation boxers that we applaud these days and I was extremely proud of him. For many years I lived in his shadow and instead of being George Gleed, I was known as 'George Gleed's boy'. It was all rather confusing, because there were three generations of us on Father's side all named George William, and even my maternal grandfather was named George Henry.

George Gleed (Brownshill)

George Gleed Senior.

Church

I was christened, confirmed and married in Bisley Church. All going well, I shall be buried here as well.

Gwen Millin (Bisley)

Ascension Day in Bisley

We used to practise marching for Ascension Day in the playground with our headmaster, 'Boss' Magor, as we used to call him. Then, on Sunday, we would go and collect the moss

for the six-sided figures and the word Ascension, which had to go on before you put the flowers on. We'd put the moss on on Monday and on Tuesday we collected the flowers. We had a very strict schoolteacher called Miss Nation and if she said it had to be yellow and blue flowers, yellow and blue it was, that was Miss Nation. Occasionally, we were allowed to go around to the big houses such as The Chantry to see if they could help out. We used to go along the vicarage garden and water the flowers on Thursday mornings. On the day, Mr Magor said he would give a prize for the one who marched the best, but then we'd go to school next day and he'd end up by giving us a penny each, which was quite a lot in those days. We had sports in the field at night and prizes for the three-legged race.

Gwen Millin (Bisley)

William Banyard, my grandfather, was the gardener for Reverend Clay at the vicarage in Bisley and he used to wind the church clock. When we had Ascension Day the people from Eastcombe used to come over on a cart – it was really a big day for us. My grampy used to get right up on the wells and put the letters AD and the year on top. The wells were all decorated with flowers, the word Ascension, five hoops to go on the waterspouts and loads of little bunches of flowers around the bottom. We would then have a tea up in the Institute and generally games up in the pleasure ground too, but it nearly always rained! So, we used to have to have it on the following Monday. It was a big day in Bisley – it still is.

Muriel Hunt (Bisley)

Sunday best

Mother was very religious. We were always made to go to church every Sunday morning, Sunday afternoon was Sunday School and then she would take us to church at night. She always went to church on Sunday nights and took us with her, three or four of us at a time. We always had to wear a hat and keep a best dress for Sundays, different to what we wore in the week. Mother used to make all our clothes. I always remember, one time she made me a coat out of a costume and a dress to match. I thought I was so smart having everything to match.

Phyllis Smith (Bisley)

From sunset Friday to sunset Saturday...

We used to go to church on a Saturday. The Seventh Day Adventist church is still along Chalford High Street opposite the Red Lion pub. In those days it was twice on a Saturday. Seventh Day Adventists keep from sunset Friday till sunset Saturday, and we did nothing. We didn't even open a letter. The milkman was cancelled, and that was a holy, a very holy day. You didn't cook; everything was done before sunset on Friday. And so you really didn't do anything, but you went to church. And you only read your bible, or religious books. On Saturday afternoon, after church, we would all go for a walk, most of the church. I used to be dressed up, oh, I used to hate it! I always had Sabbath clothes and all the children along the village would be waiting for me to come along, in this little hat and these gloves and a handbag and everything. I'd go along and they'd all be making faces at me, trying to make us laugh and I'd have to go to church and back again.

Rosie Franklin (Chalford)

Three times on a Sunday

My grandmother, Granny Clissold, lived with us and we had to go to church with her three times on a Sunday. She was very strict and, if we talked, she had some little white peppermints with three little Xs on, which she would put in our mouths to make us shut up! Sometimes, we were allowed to stay and watch the christenings, all of us Sunday School children turning round in our seats; we used to really enjoy that. There was a Miss Williams in the village who ran a Bible class. As you got older, you had to go, once a week, to this Bible class and, eventually, I become a Bible class teacher, right up to the time I was married. I'm not saying I was

Ascension Day at Bisley Wells in 1929. (copyright Express Newspapers)

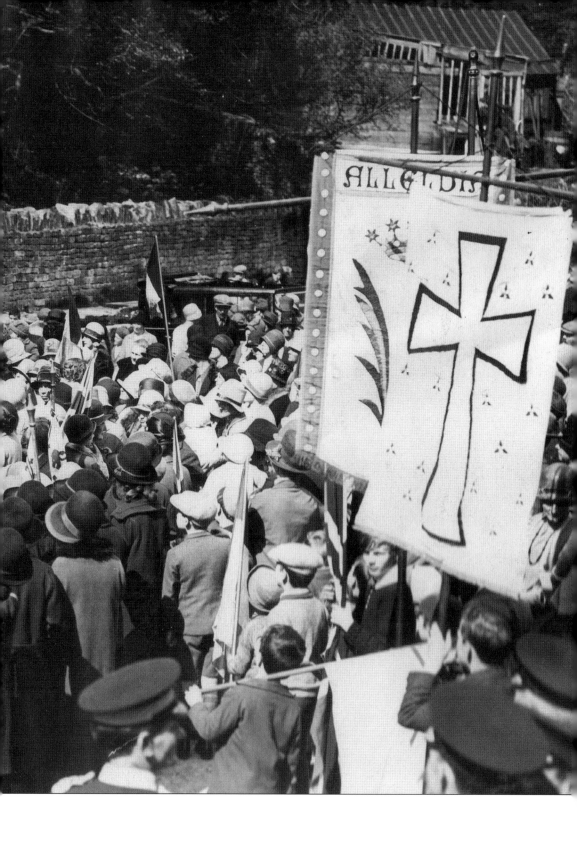

The Reverend Clay, Vicar of Bisley, with his wife.

religious, it was just how I was brought up; but on the other hand, it doesn't do any harm to go to church.

Gwen Millin (Bisley)

When I was a kiddie, I used to have to go and blow the organ. It was supposed to be Granny Clissold's job – she used to do the oil lamps and blow the organ on Sundays, morning and evening – but, of course, she got old and she would sit in with me in this little place all curtained off and I'd have to blow the organ, when it was needed. It's a handle, and you just push it up and down. I did that morning and night and went to Sunday School in the afternoon.

Hilda Ruther (Bisley)

Three times I went to church on a Sunday – it was expected. I wasn't allowed to go out to play on a Sunday, oh no! My one treat was to go out walking with my granny, down by the Wells, right down to the Chantry and on down round, coming up a little lane to the Pike. That was my treat, after church on a Sunday night.

Muriel Hunt (Bisley)

The Daffodil Wedding

If we went to church, my mum and us went to St Augustine's Church in Eastcombe, not the Baptist church, and very often we would walk up to Bisley Church. We used to walk up through the fields in the summer, but you had to walk on the roads in the winter. The vicar at Bisley then was the Reverend Clay; he was a good man. He used to come over here and teach us on alternate Sunday afternoons, and on the other Sunday, one of the sisters from the orphanage next door, St Elizabeth's, would take us. He was a good vicar. His wife, Mrs Clay, was my godmother. I've still got my Bible and the letter she sent me for my confirmation. She also stood to my brother. They had two daughters, Ruby and Margaret. Margaret married a Captain Sheppard from The Grove in Chalford. And Mum and us, we went to the wedding. That was a very grand affair; they called it the 'Daffodil Wedding' – everything was in green and yellow. Then in the evening we went to Bisley and had a tea.

Grace Winstone (Eastcombe)

The following is an extract from an eye-witness account of the society wedding at Bisley Church. It is not credited, but it is thought that it may have been sent to interested parties, unable to attend, or perhaps to the press.

A very pretty wedding in
Gloucestershire, Bisley.
4 February 1925

Captain Claud John Lorraine
Sheppard, M.C.
to
Miss Margaret de Horne
Chetwynd-Clay

The old village of Bisley had been full of interest for some weeks past in preparation for the wedding of the vicar's elder daughter who had been brought up there since she was fourteen months old, and was known by all the villagers. People were astir early in the morning and everyone wished for fine weather. The dawn broke bright and sunny, and the birds were singing. Only a few drops of rain fell just before the bride left the vicarage for the church, and then somebody kindly said, 'Oh, it is lucky to have a little rain!' Flags were flying everywhere. The villagers and many from surrounding districts were arriving in the old churchyard an hour or so before the ceremony, which was fixed for two o'clock. The church has a fine peal of eight bells, and the bell-ringers were all so keen and had managed to get time off to ring. A merry peal started at a quarter past one.

The church, which holds 500, was full some time before the service, and many could not get in. The chancel and altar had been most exquisitely decorated by many kind friends with arums and palms, etc., kindly lent from Lypiatt Park. A very effective rustic arch had been arranged at the Chancel step, where the bridal pair stood for the first part of the service: it was covered with moss, snowdrops, creepers, etc., all of which toned so beautifully with the white-robed choristers; every one had made a special effort to attend – several of them were girls dressed in white with white tulle veils. The men, the boys and the girls who sang so well and so fervently all deserve a great share of praise, and everyone present pronounced the singing perfect.

The bridegroom and his brother, Mr Lionel Sheppard – who acted as best man – were in their places in good time, the best man carrying out all his duties to perfection. The bride's mother arrived next, dressed in a powder blue chiffon velvet gown, a grey stole fur with a spray of pale pink carnations on same, and a black chiffon velvet hat with powder blue aigrette to match; she was escorted by Mr Thompson Close (cousin).

Opposite: *A society wedding at Bisley Church: The bride and groom are Captain Claud Sheppard and Miss Margaret Clay.*

Above: *Bisley villagers at the wedding.*

Then followed four bridesmaids who remained in the porch to await the arrival of the bride – Miss Betty Hossell, Miss Monica Thornton, Miss Rita Langhorne. (Miss Jean Collingridge, who was to have been one, was prevented by illness). Miss Ruby Clay, sister of the bride and Miss Doris Sheppard, sister of the bridegroom, acted as chief bridesmaids and carried the bride's train. Their dresses were very charming – almond green georgette trimmed with gold lace, caps of gold leaves and gold net, gold shoes and stockings to match the frocks. They carried beautiful bouquets of daffodils and asparagus fern tied with pale yellow ribbon to match the palest petals of the daffodils. They were all very pretty girls and made a charming bevy of bridesmaids.

Members of the Bisley choir who sang at the wedding of Captain Claud Sheppard and Margaret Clay in February 1925.

6 Chalford Station
and the Famous Rail Motor Service

The GWR and the Rail Motor service

The railway station wasn't put in Chalford to start with, because the engines weren't strong enough to pull away on the gradient. The original station was at Brimscombe opposite the King and Castle. That station was opened in August 1897; it was just ordinary trains to start with, but in October 1903, the Great Western Railway started the rail motor service. It ran from Chalford to Stonehouse. The engine was in the carriage. They ran on until the 1920s, but they weren't really powerful enough and they brought the old push-pull train in which ran on until 30 October 1964. It was packed. My wife travelled to Gloucester on it every morning. Then, Dr Beeching decided it wasn't making any money, which was a lie. The station closed on the Saturday night and on the Monday morning they started knocking it down. The contracts for the demolition were out even before the consultation was finished!

Michael Mills (Chalford)

The Brimscombe bankers

I knew all the men on the railcar: Fred Furley the ticket collector, Dave Pearce the driver. From the Brimscombe banker, we used to get lumps of coal falling down the bank. A lot of it was steam coal but sometimes there was what we called Spear's coal – that was the ultimate, the supreme coal of the period. It was flung down most of the time. I heard it said that the heavy goods trains and passenger trains would burns six tons of coal between Cheltenham and Kemble – but they wouldn't burn that much on the rest of the way to London because it was all downhill. But to Kemble it was such a gradient, all uphill, and they needed the Brimscombe bankers. When you got to Sapperton Tunnel there was such music between the two engines when they wanted some help – 'Whoop whoop, Help me! Help me!' and 'Toot, toot! I'm doing what I can!' was what you would hear!

Michael Tanner (Chalford)

A ride on the footplate

My grandfather, Signalman Harry Grimmett, was a very good railwayman, very conscientious, as they were in those days. The Great Western Railway buttons on his waistcoat always all shone up and his boots shone up too. In the 1950s, when he was working on a Sunday, we used to take his cooked dinner down in the car to him at Brimscombe. 'Have a go on the lever son', he'd say, 'Pull the lever to make the signals go'. Then he'd get on the telephone and he'd say to Mr Mills, who had the Brimscombe banker, 'There's a train coming through at such and such a time, you got room for my grandson?' And we'd have a trip up through Chalford on the footplate of the banker, right the way through Sapperton

The Chalford rail car on the 'up' platform in Chalford in around 1964.

A steam train crossing the viaduct through Chalford Valley, c. 1900.

Signalman Harry Grimmett, c. 1916.

Tunnel, where the train would go on and the banker came back. I often used to shovel the coal on and pull the whistle. As soon as you walked on to that footplate it was an experience.

Graham Mayo (Chalford)

Taking the railcar to work

I've been to Chalford station many times, particularly when it was bad weather and the Oakridge bus couldn't come. You used to walk from Waterlane down to Chalford to get the railcar to work in Stroud, so you'd done a hard slog before you'd even got there! In my parents' day, they always used Chalford station and thought nothing of walking up to Oakridge.

Yvonne Crew (Waterlane)

A busy station

Chalford station used to have two or three porters; it was a busy station during the war. If a passenger train came in and there was a lot of luggage to go on, we'd help do that, as children. We just did it because we enjoyed it.

83

Graham Mayo with his mother, Irene, in 2003. (Photograph by Peta Bunbury)

Mr Vials was the stationmaster then. We used to go up there and collect train numbers; we'd sit on the platform and wait for a train to come through. As soon as it came round the corner, you could tell by the front of it what it was. The Castle Class trains were all named after different castles around the country; then there was Hall Class and Grange Class. We never got the King's Class here because the rails were a different size. You used to have a little book and it had all the names in there. Once you'd spotted one, you'd mark if off in red or black ink to show you'd seen it.

Aston Down made the station very busy too. They used to come down and pick up a gang of airmen that had been posted there. There was a cattle yard at Chalford, which was where the Valley Trading used to be. Day Crew used to get the cattle there from Ireland: he used to come down and drive them up the hill to Westley Farm. There was a big coal wharf there too and you could watch that from our house, Station View, because Great Western used to keep all the trees trimmed back.

Graham Mayo (Chalford)

Every little village had a halt

I always think I've got some connection with the railway. My great-grandfather worked on that railway – he helped build it – but I don't know what he did. That railway viaduct for instance, that was built of timber first of all, and then they bricked round. Maybe he was a brickie. He worked on the railway, then moved down to Lydney and was buried in Cinderford churchyard.

In those days, every little village had a halt: from Stroud the train went to Bowbridge, then Brimscombe Bridge, then Brimscombe, then St Mary's, then Chalford and the next one up was Kemble. They were steam trains, not these diesels. I used to know the names of the engines and what time they ran. On the front of the engines they had little lights and each engine had a light in a different place for what sort of train it was: on the express there was one light on the top, on a luggage there were two on the outside buffers, I think it was, and the fast freight had one on the top and

one on the side. We used to take the keys off sardine tins and put them on the line to have them squashed out – just for fun.

Norman Rogers (Chalford)

Up the hill to Westley Farm

The Crew family home was Westley Farm at Chalford. It was mostly a holding centre because Norman's grandfather, Albert, was a dealer. He dealt with horses, cattle, sheep and maybe pigs. Norman's grandfather used to get cattle over from Ireland; they came via Fishguard on the train. They were taken off at Chalford station and driven up the hill to Westley Farm. This was all quite normal. Everyone knew the times of the milk trains and all the farmers who produced milk at home took their churns down to the station for it to go on the milk train to supply London. In 1936 not many people had motorised transport, so it was all done by horse and trap. Norman's father served in the

Chalford station in 1910 showing the cattle pens originally used by Albert Crew.

war, working with horses. He never wanted a tractor and always relied on horse-power to deliver the milk. Norman's father never learned to drive.

Yvonne Crew (Waterlane)

The Chalford Railcar and the fate of the Rail Motor Shed

On the night of 8 January 1916, the last rail-car in service was No.48 on the half past ten ex-Gloucester which arrived at Chalford at a quarter past eleven with Chalford driver Harold Gubbins at the controls. Its accompanying trailer may have been No.42, but this is unconfirmed. This trailer was left on the spur coupled to No.28 in readiness for the busy first train on Monday morning. No.48 was put on shed, the fire dropped and Gubbins left for home and a day off. He later reported seeing some men in the shed and certainly on that night lights were seen and noises heard. It is possible that these men were vagrants making use of the warmth afforded by the fresh-from-duty rail motor and taking advantage of the unattended shed on a Saturday night. History has not recorded whether they were frightened off by Gubbins' arrival on shed, whether they left and returned later, or if Gubbins simply turned a blind eye to their presence.

About fifteen minutes after midnight, three local men, Walter Smith, Harry Bowns and Arthur Smart were walking home along Rack Hill on the opposite side of the valley when they saw flames emanating from the distant shed. They ran down the hill to the home of signalman Harry Grimmett in Meadow Cottages.

When Grimmett was woken he immediately went to the signal box where he telephoned Brimscombe for the assistance of a banking engine. Both rail-motor trailers on the spur were very close to the engine shed

and thus in great danger from the flames, as was a gas-tank wagon, the presence of which threatened danger to a far wider area. As a result of Grimmett's prompt action, all three vehicles were removed to safety.

The horse-drawn fire engine from Brimscombe attended but their contribution was hampered by an inadequate supply of water. Both shed and No.48 were totally destroyed by the blaze. Driver Gubbins believed that the people he saw at the shed at around half past eleven were responsible for starting the fire which may have been caused by removing the burner from one of the tail lamps on the rail motor. No one really knows, though, whether the fire was started deliberately or otherwise. Some local folk suspected the bus company of having perpetrated the deed, but this was merely humorous conjecture! £2,000-worth of damage was done, and the result was the end of a shed facility at Chalford, as no replacement was ever built.

Harry Grimmett, who had come to Chalford as Signal Porter just a few days prior to the opening of the station, was awarded a gratuity of £1 1s by the GWR and commended for 'promptitude in connection with a fire at the Motor Shed, Chalford, and arranging to remove rail motor cars, which otherwise would have been destroyed'. He was promoted to Brimscombe on 13 December 1919, a much busier signal box because of the stabling of the bankers at that station. He remained there until his retirement on 9 June 1942.

Mike Fenton (extract from
British Railway Journal, Spring 1984)

Pulling a fast one

I went to the Craft School and I had to walk from Bussage to Brimscombe station every day and then go on the train to Stroud with my friend Victor. One day I went in to see the headmaster and complained. 'Look', I said, 'I have to start from home at half past seven in the morning to catch the eight o'clock train and I don't get home until late'. In the end he gave us permission to get the half past eight train and we missed our Scripture lesson. We were excused homework because we didn't get home until about a quarter past five. But the joke of it was that the Eastcombe boys had to walk through Bussage to get to Brimscombe, but they didn't get let off! The two of us could walk in at about a quarter past nine! I shouldn't have pulled a fast one, but when you're that age it's the name of the game!

Brian Beavis (Bussage)

A kind stationmaster

In the mid 1950s the stationmaster at Chalford station was called Nat Ollerenshaw. He was such a nice person – he was tall and his uniform was always pristine. Each morning I used to cycle from the Valley Inn, where I lived, to catch the five to eight railcar to Gloucester, where I was working as a secretary. He'd stand up on the goods yard and he could look down onto the towpath as far as the Red Lion and beyond. He knew exactly who was catching the morning railcar and if he could see that I was running behind he'd call, 'Leave your bike down there and I'll come and fetch it for you when you're gone' and he'd hold the railcar for me. Every morning catching the railcar with me from Chalford were Graham Mayo, Philly Baglin,

Keith Peacey and Arthur Rowles from Oakridge, Trevor Smith and David Freeman. When the railcar stopped, Graham used to take four of us to Gloucester in his Morris Minor.

Jean Tanner (Chalford)

Tunnel gangs in the natives' room

On a Sunday there weren't many passenger trains and the tunnel gangs would come out. If there was a good ganger on in those days he would come to the Chalford end of the tunnel or he would go up the Daneway end. There were two pubs – the Daneway and the Valley. We used to silently open the back door of the Valley so that the railwaymen didn't all come in at one go because there could have been fifteen or twenty in a gang as well as the normal clients on a Sunday. They always used what we called the 'natives' room', and even though we were going to have a cooked Sunday lunch, they'd have meat in a red and white dotted handkerchief spread out like a table cloth and a great lump of cheese and a raw onion. They would have a penknife in their pocket and slice a piece off; it was really appetising to see them sit down and eat like that. I've often thought I could eat that meal – the cooked dinner wouldn't worry me. Then they'd have a couple of pints and get back to work.

They use to tap the rail – they knew if there was a sleeper loose or if there was something out of line, and the GWR was the safest railway in England.

Michael Tanner (Chalford)

A view of the Valley Inn, Chalford, c. 1910, also showing the railway viaduct and the Valley Lock in the foreground.

7 Barges on the Thames and Severn Canal

The barge donkeys

I can remember the barges coming up when I was a girl. We used to run down to watch the barges and the poor old donkeys pulling them up the canal. They had donkeys because horses were too big for the towpath. In some parts they used to have to board the donkeys because there wasn't a towpath and the men had to pole the barges. The donkeys knew when they had to stop and they would go no further; they were stubborn as mules! There was always a space left for the two donkeys in the coal barge. They would jump up on to the platform, tearing up there to get into the barge. They knew what to do; they were intelligent.

We weren't allowed to play on the canal side because it was very deep and there were several children drowned in the locks. One was one of the Dean children from what we used to call 'Ducks Nest' under Hyde Hill. One was a Padin – Lionel's brother Claude – he was lost in the lock, and there was another boy drowned at Thrupp, Brian Bond. We weren't allowed to go, but our garden at Belvedere ran right down to the canal where I lived. You were frightened off it.

Mabel Smith (Chalford)

Pulling the lock gate

I had a very, very happy childhood, a lot of love and plenty to eat and I was quite relaxed in that house in Meadow Cottages. There were eight children in the houses along there and we used to all play together. And when a barge came along the canal there was a lock gate and we would all say 'Oh, here's a barge coming up, my turn to pull the lock gate', and the ones who didn't pull it would sit on it and have the ride. The people on the boat would have had to do it if we hadn't done it. The boats would go up to Sapperton and back down. They didn't have horses though. There was a lock right behind my house and my father worked in the signal box straight up the wall. My father, Harry Grimmett, was the signalman for the railway and he could see us pulling the lock gate.

Irene Mayo (Chalford)

Jumping on a timber barge

I rode on a barge once. I wasn't supposed to, mind, but he was passing through a lock and I jumped on. Some builders were cutting trees down and they couldn't get them out, apart from getting them on a barge. So they brought over a timber barge. There was a difference between a timber barge and a coal barge: a timber barge had wider gunwales, and it was heavier built. When they were going through the lock gates, we jumped on and rode for about 150 yards. It must have been a special thing, though, because whatever we was doing, we'd always stop and say, 'Ooh look, there's a barge coming up.' If they had come

A card postmarked 1921 showing a working barge on the canal.

A view of the canal behind Chalford station, c. 1912. Meadow Cottages, where Irene Mayo lived as a child, are the second and third houses backing on to the canal path, on the left. The signal box is opposite Meadow Cottages, across Clowes Bridge and up the bank.

The Valley Lock, Chalford, c. 1910, with what is now the Valley Playing Field on the left.

up every hour we wouldn't have taken any notice, but we did.

Norman Rogers (Chalford)

The bargees and the 'tell-tale'

The barges used to come up to unload the coal. It took them a long time, because everything was done by hand. There were tons of coal on one barge. Women lived on there with their husbands. When they came to Chalford they would get on the drink, because they'd been a long time coming 'ashore'. They'd want to play cards with the locals in the Company's Arms, and every night, until they got the coal unloaded, they'd be in there. My uncle kept the pub – he was a widower, and my mother used to help him.

I was with my mother one day and she was talking to someone who asked, 'What happened to the tell-tale?' Of course, I cocked my ears. 'Oh,' she said, 'We took it down to

have some decorating done and we put it on a shelf and it got broken.' Well, the 'tell-tale' was like a mirror on the ceiling for the card-sharpers. The locals knew it was there. They'd get the bargees to play with them and, of course, all the time they were reading their cards!

A lot of people don't realise, but if you're going from Chalford to Sapperton, if you go up Cowcombe Hill – it's a steep hill, that is – by the time the canal gets up there, they meet up on the top road. It's marvellous really. They say the break in the tunnel is as high as St Paul's Cathedral.

Mabel Smith (Chalford)

No money, only tokens

The Thames and Severn Canal used to have tokens: the bargees didn't have money until they got off the trip. They never had any money, they would only spend the tokens and

The Company's Arms, Chalford, in the mid-1930s. One of the oldest buildings in the area and no longer a pub, it is now a private residence called Chalford Place and is undergoing major renovation.

then the barge owner would know where they'd spent their tokens. It was no good them saying they'd gone to Frampton when they'd stopped at the Valley.

Michael Tanner (Chalford)

Tubby Franklin and the barge donkeys

Tubby Franklin used to look after the barge donkeys when they came to port. When the barges finished, they took the donkeys up and Tubby had them for good in his meadows. He used to sell those donkeys and he'd say, 'If he comes back to me, you can't have him back and you can't have your money back, either.' One donkey kept coming back to him – he sold it about six times! In the end, he sold it to someone far away so it couldn't keep coming back.

Mabel Smith (Chalford)

A hard life as a bargee

Bargees used to go down to a coal merchant and get the barge and the barge owner would give him a sum of money. Then he'd take the barge up to Staffordshire, load up and go through locks. If he had to pay through a lock, he had to pay out, or if he was towed up the Severn, he had to pay out. If he had to be helped to load on, he'd pay out then as well, and he had to repeat it on his journey back. It would take him about twelve days to go up there and back. Any money he got left was his wage; it could be as low as fifteen shillings for a fortnight's work. Well, if you were a married man with a couple of kids, that wasn't a lot of money. Those people did survive, but it was hard going.

Norman Rogers (Chalford)

Donkeys by the side of the canal.

8 Wartime
'They shall not pass'

German prisoners

Towards the end of the war, the wood behind Cowcombe Hill was cut down by German prisoners. As children, we used to go up over the bridge and, where the escape road is now, there was a big wooden shed or workshop where a fellow called Smith used to do woodworking. He used to let it out to the powers that be for the German prisoners. They would all congregate there for their cups of tea and their meal. We got friendly with a chap we nicknamed 'Cookie', a little chap with a moustache and a German hat; he could speak a little bit of English and we used to get through to him. His party trick was that he had a tree trunk that lay horizontal and he would get on that tree trunk and go horizontal on one hand – he'd do that every time we went up. Around lunch time, you'd see all these Germans come down Cowcombe Hill and have their cup of tea. Some were friendly, some weren't.

A lot of them – a few hundred – were at Aston Down. We used to play cricket and football with them as kids, but we had to pack up playing cricket with them, because they never had a clue. Germans don't play cricket, and instead of bowling they would throw. It got a little bit dangerous for us, as youngsters!

As time went on – 1946, 1947 – they began to drift home. They had a little bit more freedom then, and they used to come round the village trying to sell things they'd made, like shoes. Of course, we was always told not to have anything to do with them, which we didn't really, apart from going up there, but we'd never speak to them if they walked through the village.

Graham Mayo (Chalford)

Americans at Lypiatt Park

By the time I was fourteen in 1944 there were hundreds of American soldiers in the area and a large encampment of them at Lypiatt Park. Some of the men used to come over to the Ram Inn at Bussage for a drink. Occasionally, people used to grumble about them, but they were really kind and generous. They would give us candy, gum and tins of peaches; all items that were unobtainable in the normal way. Many of them were only three or four years older than us boys. I remember my sister, Mavis, had a Yankee boyfriend, but he was posted to another part of the country. One day she was reading a paper when, to her horror, she read that he had been involved in some crime, tried and hanged! It upset her badly and she confided in my sister and myself, but kept it from Mum and Dad.

Then one day, the Yanks arrived for a drink with close-cropped hair ready for the invasion of France on D-Day and we never saw any of them again. I still think about them at times and wonder how many survived.

George Gleed (Brownshill)

A pair of nylons

The Americans came to Lypiatt, and that was quite something. They were there for D-Day, I think. They had nylons and everything! The girls thought it was wonderful, if they could get a pair of nylons! They were so different. I had a few American boyfriends, before I met Stan, of course! They used to get to all the dances and everything. Of course, they had transport, the Americans.

Pam Turner (France Lynch)

Aston Down

Aston Down was a proper RAF camp – a lot of flying. There were huts then, it's not like it is now. The road you come along from Minchinhampton, that road was incorporated in the camp. To get from Minchinhampton to Cirencester you had to go down Hyde Hill and up the Cowcombe Hill. Aston Down was actually built in the First World War – it housed a lot of Australians. It got bigger during the Second World War as it was a place for training pilots.

Graham Mayo (Chalford)

The Junkers 88 crash

I remember as a schoolboy at Chalford Hill School hearing about the German plane which crashed over at France Lynch, a Junkers 88. Two of us went over (we should have been on our way home from school), and eventually we found the wreckage and I came home with an aluminium panel with six switches on and that was a trophy that hung in the shed for donkey's years; it must have been there for twenty or thirty years!

I remember standing on the recreation ground and seeing the puffs and shell-bursts of a German plane flying across at the height of five or six thousand feet; it was excitement in those days.

David Collins (Bussage)

One day in 1940 we were in the playground at school when an air battle took place, not directly overhead, but within sight. For once, the headmaster lost control of us because, although he tried to order us inside the school, we refused to go even though he resorted to hitting out at us. The result of the action was that a British Hurricane Fighter crashed at Oakridge and a German Junkers 88 crashed in the Strawberry Banks between Oakridge and France Lynch. As soon as school was over, we nearly all raced over to see the German plane and get pieces of it for souvenirs. I remember getting into deep trouble for being late home from school.

George Gleed (Brownshill)

We had a Junkers 88 crash in July 1940 over in the Strawberry Banks or Bidcombe's as it's properly called. They had armed officers and some airmen there from Aston Down guarding it. Why they were guarding it, I don't know. Anyway, George Juggins arrived up there with his bowler hat and his silver-headed cane on the Saturday morning and said to the officer, 'Good morning, my man', and the officer thought it was the local squire and proceeded to show George round! Of course, everybody was standing round laughing their heads off! George had a nerve for anything.

That was a seven-day wonder, that plane. It crashed on 25 July 1940. They ran buses from Stroud to bring people up to see it. I can remember seeing it come down, because we were all at school. It was rammed by a Hurricane. The Hurricane crashed at Oakridge, and all they found was bits of the pilot. One of the Junkers' engines fell out by Pontings Farm and the plane crashed down by

George Juggins outside his cottage.

Bidcombe's: you can still see the patch of ground where it landed as it's a lot greener than the rest. The crew jumped out, but one man's parachute didn't open. He was buried with full military honours at Brimscombe Cemetery. He was in the top of a tree. My dad led the search party round the wood to find him. They moved his body after the war to the German Cemetery at Cannock Chase. Round here in the war, there were crashes almost every week.

Michael Mills (Chalford)

I remember the German plane coming down in the fields by Oakridge. I remember, at the time, we had an airman's wife staying here and the airman was here too. We saw it coming down and he took me to the Oakridge fields; and I remember the German up in the trees in the parachute. It was very sad, but it wasn't frightening, because he couldn't have done anything, could he?

Pam Turner (France Lynch)

Harry Herrmann and Chalford AFC

Harry Herrmann was a German Prisoner of War who, when he was released at the end of the war, decided to stay on in England. He found himself work at the nurseries down the Stonehouse Road, but for many years he came up to Chalford to play in goal for Chalford Football Club. He was a very popular bloke and he used to play several other sports when he was here. He eventually went back home to Germany and got married, but he's been coming back here every few years ever since, and the old football team have a get-together. He made very good friends around the Stonehouse and Stroud areas as well as in Chalford and he really values the years of friendship shown to him by the members of Chalford Football team and their wives.

Derek Shergold (Chalford)

Chalford AFC in 1949/50. From left to right, back row: Ron Davis, Tony Davis, Percy Abel, -?-, Harry Herrmann, Derek Shergold, Freddie Hayward, Len Kibble, Ernie Young, John Barnes. Front row: Mr Freeman (the bath man), Frank Gardiner, Des Gardiner, Colin Godwin, Harry Allen, Les Kirby, Colin Davis.

Forty years on in 1990, Harry Herrmann comes back to meet up with his old team mates at the Mechanics Arms (now The Old Neighbourhood, in Chalford Hill). From left to right: Ron Goodship, Frank Gardiner, Tony Davis, Les Kirby, Des Gardiner, Mrs Herrmann, Harry Herrmann, Ernie Young, Derek Shergold, Colin Godwin.

Building a shelter

Initially, no one really knew what was going to happen, and at the beginning everyone took their own precautions. I remember that Dad and a couple of other local men decided that the bottom of our garden should be turned into an air-raid shelter, and so it was. They dug a huge hole, covered it over with logs and roofed it with corrugated iron with earth piled on top of it. It had seats in and there was room for about a dozen people. It got used, occasionally, but it was used for storage in the end. It had its own entrance from the road and was quite a structure, really. It was quite clean, if a bit damp.

David Collins (Bussage)

They Shall Not Pass

Dave Collins' father, Bill, built an air-raid shelter during the war. In fact, Dave and I spent many happy hours playing in it! It was dug out at the bottom of his garden and was accessible from the road by a little doorway. It was very nice in there: it had planks inside. It never really got used, but it would have been useful had the need ever arisen. We really thought we were going to be attacked. We had roadblocks everywhere with huge pylons and telegraph posts with slogans such as 'They Shall Not Pass!' written on them to make people aware that there could be an invasion and that people would come through this area.

Peter Clissold (Bussage)

Chalford LDV

Mr David Fuller was captain of the Chalford LDV (Local Defence Volunteers) in the early 1940s, just after the Battle of Britain when we really thought the Germans were coming. Graham Mayo's father, Larry, was a sergeant in the LDV and the warning came through that 'they' were on their way. Larry Mayo lived nearest to Captain Fuller's, and because of this he was to be the 'drum' – the person that would wake everyone up in an emergency. Anyway, this night Larry heard a rattling at his door and there was Mr Fuller in a hell of a state, shouting 'They're coming, they're coming! Marshall all the men and we'll meet at the bus stop in twenty minutes' time! Bring whatever you've got in the form of ammunition.' Larry said, 'I've only got an armband', and Fuller said, 'Bring that, it'll help!' It was all in the heat of the moment! We really thought they were coming, and we never knew whether it was a genuine alarm, or whether it was designed to check the reaction of the LDV. Afterwards, they were officially recognised as the stand-back army and they were called the Home Guard.

Michael Tanner (Chalford)

Working with the Land Girls

From working in the bakehouse, I went to work in the land army out at Througham during the war; I used to ride my bike out there. I wasn't old enough to work as a land girl, but I worked with two land girls and I used to do exactly what they did, milking cows and stonewalling, picking up stones out of the fields. Once, I helped birth a cow with two heads! The vet came and tied a rope on to the ankles of the calf – it was breech – and we had to pull it out. Of course, the bailiff's wife, she'd had babies and she kept saying, 'Be careful, Rupert, don't hurt her' because she knew what the poor cow was going through. The mother lived for three months afterwards, but she had to be put down in the end. When I went home and told my mother and father what I'd done, they raised the roof to think I could have witnessed such a thing as that. My dad, Arthur Clissold, was the barber in Bisley,

David Collins in 2003.
(Photograph by Peta Bunbury)

and when the bailiff came for his haircut, I think my father had a few words with him for letting me see it. Then I went down to Tyler's along Chalford Bottom, making fuselage. Then in 1943 I got married, in Bisley Church with the two families there, the Clissolds and the Millins. My husband only had three days' leave before he had to go abroad.

Gwen Millin (Bisley)

A wartime wedding

Eventually, all the men went off to the war. My husband went in to the navy. We got married in 1944 when I was twenty-two. He was an electrical artificer. He went over on the D-Day landings and his nerves were terribly bad after that; he had to go to recuperate in Southend-on-Sea. He didn't ever want to talk about it much; it was only later on that he let some things drop. He was ready to go to the

A wartime wedding at Bisley Church in 1944 between Muriel Banyard and Kenneth Hunt.

Far East – I don't know how he got out of going, but he didn't go. Perhaps they wanted him for the D-Day.

Muriel Hunt (Bisley)

Twenty-four hours' leave to get married

I got married on 9 September 1939. We were going to be married in the October and my husband was in the territorials, but we brought it forward because he had to go as soon as war broke out. He managed to get twenty-four hours' leave to get married. He came home at two o'clock just in time to meet me at the church and he had to go the next day at midday. Then I didn't see him for six weeks. I went down to Ilfracombe where he was billeted and stopped down there with him for a month; then, of course, he was drafted all over the place. He was abroad for three years out in Egypt. Luckily, he came through without any scars or anything. Six years he did in the army. The first six years of our life together were ruined because we weren't together.

Phyllis Smith (Bisley)

William Smith, Phyllis' husband, in his uniform in 1939.

Bombs at Aston Down

My father was working nights at Fibrecrete during the war and he'd divided off part of the cellar so we had the well in one corner and the wood and coal in the other. We had a little room down there where there was a bed in one corner and, in case of air raids, my little brother, James, would be in the clothes basket and Peter and I would be put to sleep down in the cellar. I always remember the night when they actually bombed Aston Down and the men from Fibrecrete were sent home to their families. My father came home and we were locked in and my mother heard the banging on the door and went to the door with the carving knife!

Pam Clissold (Bussage)

Making frames for aeroplanes

During the war I was working at Tyler's: it was an upholsterers and they made chair frames, but during the war they made balsa-wood frames for the Mosquito aircraft. They made the wings and other smaller parts. When Father died, I was the only one bringing in the money. You had to start with seven and six a week and half a crown had to come out of

101

that for bus fares. I worked down there in peacetime as well; I did French polishing and I worked in the sanding shop.

Grace Winstone (Eastcombe)

Evacuees at the village hall

I started Bussage school at three years old: I was one of the very youngest. At the same time, all the evacuees were here. Some came from Birmingham and a lot from Clacton and all round that area. They stayed with different families in the village. We had a boy staying with us called Tommy Felton who was only five years old. They all arrived at the village hall and everyone who was prepared to take a child went to the hall and you came out with one and took them back to your house with their suitcase and all their belongings. We had no previous knowledge of the child. They were all sent to the west of England for safety because Clacton and that side were getting all the flack from the bombing. Jack Munday was one of the organisers. He was a parish councillor and church warden who helped to sort the children out. It was difficult for the evacuees to settle in and it was hard for them for a while, but they did settle and then they were very happy here, I think. There were some at Chalford School, too, when I went there. They were mostly from Clacton and Walton on the Naze, with some from Birmingham and some from London. I was an only child so my parents could take one evacuee.

Peter Clissold (Bussage)

9 Local Characters

George and Dorcas

George and Dorcas Juggins were children of the soil; they lived the way that country people had lived for years. I really always felt extremely privileged when I went there, to have seen life as it was and will never be again.

Daphne Neville (Frampton Mansell)

They adored animals but hated kids

George and Dorcas Juggins lived along Ashmeads. I grew up knowing George and Dorcas; they adored animals but they hated kids. If I was to go along and see her she'd say, 'Eh, don't you bring those bloody kids in 'ere. Make them stay out. I hate bloody kids,' she'd say, 'I love animals. When they grow old they'll never leave you. If you have kids, they always leave you'. She had a filthy mouth; she was disgusting. She used to take snuff. She used to frighten the life out of us as kids. Of course, we used to tease her, as you can imagine. She'd be on the front of the bus, stinking. George was something else: there he'd be with his bowler and his walking stick, going to the pub. He worked down the stick mill. He died one December, and in January or February I went along in the day to see her. You couldn't hear yourself speak in there. Our kids were out by the wall. There were dogs barking – they were chained to the fire grate. On the table, there was a lip all the way round and the guinea pigs ran round it. She just sat by the fire, for hour after hour, with this long hanging hair. She went to bed that night, they reckon, and knocked down the candle. She burnt to death – everything burnt.

Rosie Franklin (Chalford)

Life at Ashmeads

My grandfather bought Ashmeads Mill in 1903. It was an old silk mill; it had closed down and was partially derelict. He built a house and lived there from 1903 until he died in 1946. My grandmother had a stroke when she was sixty and she had to be looked after so he bought the mill manager's house next door for my aunt. We were the only ones along Ashmeads, apart from Dorcas and George Juggins. Dorcas originally lived in one of the cottages on my father's land. She was a Townsend; her family used to run the horse buses from Chalford to Stroud and they were quite a well-off family at one time. She was evidently a little bit strange. Their house burnt down in 1975; she went to bed with a candle and, as my uncle says, 'They brought her out on a shovel'.

Michael Mills (Chalford)

Potato-picking with Dorcas

In wartime, during the potato-picking season, we used to have to go from the school and do so many hours in the fields. We used to go to

George and Dorcas Juggins.

Stancombe, and Dorcas was working there. And being lads, we used to tease her. 'I'm not working with them buggers,' she used to say, 'If I'm staying, I'm going over there. You keep them that side'. George used to work part-time for the water board, and he used to do all the lights on the road when they did the mains water. They put a main right from the bottom up to that reservoir that you see along the Bisley road on the left, and George used to have to do the lights. Needless to say, as fast as he put the lights up, the kiddies put them out – poor George.

Harry Cadwallader (Chalford)

George and Darling Mabel

George was true blue. He always had Conservative Party posters; he had blue bows on his bicycle. That was George. He worked down at the stick factory. He worked all over.

They used to have a machine called a trapping machine that you put wood through, like two grinding wheels. George stuck his finger in when he was a boy, and my grandfather had to extract it for him. He was always very grateful to grandfather after that.

They had Dorcas' mother living there with them at one time, who was known as 'Darling Mabel'. They used to push her to Stroud in a bath chair. They had a bicycle, so one would ride off and wait for the other to catch up with the bath chair and then they'd push on and the other one would ride ahead and have a rest. One day, George was pushing her around Stroud. She was in her chair at the top of Gloucester Street, and George had a few drinks on board and he said 'Right, you b....' and he shoved her bath chair down Gloucester Street!

They used to keep the goats and other animals out on that swampy ground. One night, George had been supposed to get the

A picture of the couple to mark George's retirement from the stick factory in 1965. (Both photographs reproduced by kind permission of Mrs June Turner)

goat in, and he was wandering along, half cut, about three o'clock in the morning and Dorcas was getting the goats in the meadow. He said something to her from the road and my father had to get up and tell them to shut up for the noise they were making!

Michael Mills (Chalford)

Taking in lodgers

George and Dorcas were both a little bit simple in their way. George was crafty, mind: he always used to say he'd go home drunk on a Saturday night and he hadn't spent a penny! He always wore collars, cuffs, bowler hat and pinstriped trousers: he looked like Charlie Chaplin. But that cottage was a filthy, dirty place and, if you can imagine, they had six lodgers when they were building Aston Down in 1938. Ernie Dukes was the last one and he stayed. He came from a very well-to-do family; he was a very well-educated man who'd gone down through drink. He'd worked all over the world. He could talk to you about anything. One day, a Bentley pulled up and it was his brother, who had come looking for him. But his brother took one look at him, got in the car and drove off. He didn't want to know. Ernie was an alcoholic, but when he was sober he was a very pleasant man to talk to.

Michael Mills (Chalford)

A poor quality photograph of Dorcas (centre) and her lodger, Ernie Dukes. The lady on the left is unknown.

Ernie falls in the canal

I remember Ernie Dukes – a drunk, but a very well-travelled man. I remember when I was courting, my wife lived down at Wotton-under-Edge. I went down through the Red Lion to get on to the canal, as I was catching the three o'clock railcar into Stroud. I'd just got on to the canal and I could hear, 'Help! help!' and I thought, 'Well, what's that?' and, down the bank, in the water, was Ernie Dukes with his bike on top of him. And there was me, all spruced up ready to go courting, and I had to struggle down that bank, pull his bike up and pull him up, and he was absolutely blotto! When I eventually got up to the station I thought I'd nip into the yard and look down, and there he was, with the bike upside down on the path trying to put the chain on.

Graham Mayo (Chalford)

'They be friends of ours'

I remember George Juggins used to come up every day and get the milk. I think most people who knew George thought him trustworthy, and it was the same with Dorcas. We used to put the milk out for him. He never came until what I call bedtime, he'd come along with his lantern to collect the milk and we used to say, 'It's George, it's all right'. Nobody worried. They used to go up to Oakridge and Bisley with a pram for their shopping. They used to go to the pub in Oakridge and down to pubs in Bisley – they were part of the scene. Norman's family always treated them like you'd treat anyone else.

I suppose they knew we were getting married and they turned up at Bisley Church for our wedding. If you'd ever seen how they were dressed! It was very way out! George used to wear a bowler hat. Bruce Rand, who

George Juggins with his pram – a once familiar sight along Ashmeads and around Chalford, Oakridge and Bisley.

lived at Ridings, was one of our ushers and he knew them. They came into the church and went right up to the front. Bruce went up to them and asked if they would mind sitting at the back and Dorcas said, 'Oh no, they be friends of ours' and they sat just where my mother should have sat! This all happened before I arrived at the church. They weren't going to sit at the back! People still remind me of that today.

Yvonne Crew (Waterlane)

Looking after Dorcas

It was quite well known that George and Dorcas and the lodger Ernie Dukes shared a bed. One day, Dorcas was asked why she and George never had any children and was it George's fault, to which Dorcas immediately replied, 'Ooh no, we've had a lodger for years'.

George sadly died of heart disease in December 1974 and the powers that be wanted Dorcas to move into an old folk's

A poignant image of this extraordinary couple walking along Ashmeads to their cottage.

home. Well, there was no way she was going to do that, so she was allowed to stay in her house. There was a local councillor called Duncan Young who used to go in and do her fire for her and Mrs Ev Clark, who lived next door, and I decided that we would take it in turns to take her lunch. Dorcas also entrusted me to go and cash her allowance book.

I was very worried because she had two dogs at that stage – there was a black and white collie dog which was kept in a shed on its own and she had a sandy-coloured one which was with her at all times. And then there was the guinea pig which was on the table – there was always a guinea pig on the table. I cashed her money and bought the groceries she needed, then I saved enough money to get the collie dog spayed, then persuaded her to let me find a home for it, which I did.

The worst job, of course, was emptying the pot which was under her chair. Originally, the privy was just a hole round the back; they had never had a tap and they used to get their water from the brook. So I would trot down the valley with her lunch on a tray, and Mrs Clark very kindly allowed me to empty the pot in her lavatory. One day, I couldn't go and Mrs Clark was due to take over. When I went back, I was dreading it because I thought the pot would be really overflowing by then. So I said, 'Come on Dorcas, let me have the potty.' 'Oh, no', she said 'That's not necessary' and, indeed, the pot was empty. So I said, 'What did you do with it, Dorcas?' 'Ooh', she said 'I put it on the fire!'

People used to make fun of them in Chalford, which is why they went up to Oakridge and Bisley, and of course they loved the Butchers Arms. Dorcas used to love to call in here on the way back and use our lavatory!

Daphne Neville (Chalford)

The death of Ernie Dukes

Ernie Dukes was a Canadian – he was quite an educated man until he got near licensed premises. Cider was his downfall. Way back in 1952 or 1953 he was seriously ill and he went into the Delancey Hospital in Cheltenham. In those days, if you went in there you weren't expected to come out upright. Dorcas and George in their sympathy and concern went and fetched him out of there – they wanted to look after him. They didn't want to go to Cheltenham on the double-decker bus to see him, they wanted to look after him at home. The hospital authorities didn't have the power to keep him.

The sewer was coming up the canal at that time. Dorcas and George went over to Cheltenham and they got Dukes out. He could hardly stand, but they got him out in fits and starts on to the double-decker at Cheltenham and over to Stroud, then on the Chalford bus to the Central Garage at the bottom of Cowcombe Hill – and that meant a long walk along the canal to where they lived at Ashmeads. It was a Saturday lunchtime and we received news at the Valley Inn that Dorcas and George were bringing Ernie Dukes up the canal path. There was a firm called Rees and Son who were the contractors doing the sewers up through Chalford, and every few yards there was a little tarpaulin hut where you had a barrel with planks on where you could shelter from the weather – they managed to get Ernie into the first one which was very near Meadow Cottages. The next one was round the Narrows, and we said we'd better go down and offer to help them – we couldn't just look out of the window. So I went and got a brandy and went down the canal and there was Dukes. He didn't had enough breath to blow a candle out; he was sat there and I thought he was dying. We gave him this sip of brandy; he coughed and spluttered, but it revived him temporarily, and because he showed a bit of life, Dorcas said, 'Come on, we'll make for home again.' They managed to get him home because they didn't have to go up any hills; they could go straight up the tow path.

They got him home and, after a couple of days, they sent for Dr Middleton, who told them that Ernie was desperately ill but that he would be in attendance whenever they wanted him. (He was a hero, ENC Middleton; he was a very good doctor). Dorcas sent a message along to me asking if I would go and see Ernie Dukes. Jean said, 'You're not going in there!' I had been in there before: wire netting around the kitchen table, day-old chicks under the kitchen table, the dogs on the settee... Anyway, I went.

George said, 'C..c..c...come on then, Mike,' (he had a terrible stutter, did George), and I put my foot through the first step of the stairs going up. No electric, no gas, just torchlight to go up the stairs and into Dukes'. We got into the bedroom – I could hardly stand up straight – and there was a bed with the *London Illustrated*, *Home*, *Picture Post* and all the magazines of that period, a bit of rug and a bit of something else. That was all there was on the bed. There were no blankets, but there's a lot of heat in paper and cardboard. George put the torch on and said 'Look, th...th...th...there he is Mike,' but he didn't know who I was, and I felt a bit sad going up there, really. But I'd done what Dorcas and George wanted me to do.

The following night, they had to send for Dr Middleton. He stayed there for three hours and even ate a bacon sandwich in there! Not many people would do that, because it was a black hob and the bread was handled after feeding the chickens or whatever. Dr Middleton stayed until Ernie died, then he went back on the hill. That was an act of extreme comfort to George and Dorcas, because they wouldn't have known if Ernie was dead or alive left to themselves.

Michael Tanner (Chalford)

George with television presenter Bruce Hockin and Daphne Neville at the Neville's Water Carnival, held at Bakers Mill in the summer of 1967.

WOMAN DIES IN BLAZING HOUSE

A Chalford woman believed to be nearly eighty years of age, was burned to death when her house caught fire on Friday night.

The body of Mrs Dorcas Juggins, of Ashmeads Cottage, Chalford, was discovered by firemen after they had fought to bring the fire under control.

Mrs Juggins had lived alone in the house since the death of her husband George in December. Both were well known throughout the Stroud district.

The Fire Service was called to the house by a neighbour. Mr Reginald Clarke had been aroused by his wife to find the house well alight. He got into his car and drove along the Valley Road to the nearest telephone box where he contacted the Fire Service.

A police spokesman said the firemen reached the house at about half past two on Friday morning, but when they arrived, the premises were already burning furiously.

The flames were eventually brought under control and firemen used breathing apparatus to search the wreckage.

Mrs Juggins' body was found in a bedroom about three hours later.

On Saturday morning, police and Fire Service experts were still trying to find out the cause of the blaze. Foul play is not suspected.

The Cheltenham District Coroner, Mr K.O. Brooks, ordered that a inquest be opened on Mrs Juggins at Stroud yesterday (Wednesday) following a post mortem examination.

Stroud News and Journal,
27 February 1975

Sidney Stares' and the shaking scissors

Mr and Mrs Stares were the old people that ran the shop at the top side of the Duke of York in Chalford Hill. It were a lovely grocer's shop and you could place bets there as he used to be the local bookie. They had two sons and a daughter. Their son, Sidney Stares, had something like Parkinson's disease. He used to work in the sweet shop and they used to have rows of sweets in jars there during the war. Of course, you used to have to give in your coupons, and he had to cut the little D or C out, and his old scissors were shaking! You were frightened to death he was going to cut the wrong square out! And that was poor Sidney, and he used to look after the shop. They used to keep pigs and bake bread in the old premises, as far as I remember.

Harry Cadwallader (Chalford)

A drawer full of sovereigns

Holmes used to have a grocer's shop in the valley where Noah's Ark is now. They closed the bottom one and they brought everything up to Chalford Hill – all the shop fittings and everything. That's when she gave me a gold sovereign. I said she shouldn't be so kind, and she said, 'Muriel, we've got hundreds of them'. They had a false drawer in the bottom of the cash drawer and it were full of gold sovereigns. 'Whenever there's anybody I like I give them one', she said.

Muriel Cadwallader (Chalford)

The Holmes of Chalford post office

Miss Holmes used work in the Chalford Hill Post Office. The counter was exactly where it is now. You would go in and she used to fold her arms and talk to you for half an hour, and even if you kept looking round she wouldn't take a tinker's notice of anybody. You could go, as far as she was concerned. If she folded her arms and leant against the fireplace, that was that. You'd be walking backwards, trying to get away from her.

She was from a big family with a lot of children. One Sunday, this boy came for some treacle, (they used to sell golden treacle by the jug). He knocked at the back door and said, 'Can I have twopence worth of treacle, Mr Holmes?' And Mr Holmes said 'This is Sunday and we don't normally serve, but I will do just this once', and he snatched the boy's jug off him and went into the outhouse and got him his treacle. Then he said, 'Come on then, twopence please' and the boy says, 'It's at the bottom of the jug, Mister'. Miss Holmes said she thought her father was going to kill him. She said, 'We sat round the table and we daren't laugh, but it was so funny!'.

Harry Cadwallader (Chalford)

An absolute riot

Blanche Young was a teacher up at France Lynch School and a friend of mine. Olive Cresswell was her junior. She taught there. We were at the High School together, actually, then Olive came and taught here. Blanche was an absolute riot, she really was. She taught us at Sunday School as well. She used to lend me books. She had a brother, Ernie, who was in the choir. He was a very difficult man, but he had the most lovely tenor voice. In those days we had a wonderful choir at St John the Baptist in France Lynch; there were several men with really good voices. And of course, there were the Hallidays: Albert, Margery and Doris. They all had lovely voices. Margery played the organ at the children's service and Doris ran the Brownies.

Florence Workman (France Lynch)

Mrs Stares standing in front of her sweet shop in around 1915-20. The shop became Pincott's Stores and finally a private residence in 1988.

A wonderful woman

Blanche Young was such a character. She taught at the school and she'd had some nursing experience. Blanche was good when Stan's mother used to have blackouts, it was so soothing, really. She said to my mother once, 'Now, when you die, Muriel, you mustn't die on a Monday, because the vicar teaches on a Monday.' And do you know? She died herself on a Monday! She used to lay people out; she was a wonderful woman. She was the agent for the Children's Society. That's how all these children came here for adoption. Blanche never had children herself – she was Sunday School superintendent. We always had to learn our collects every Sunday and if we didn't do it properly we had to learn two for the following Sunday.

Another thing about Blanche – she used to knit for Peyton and Baldwin's, who did the knitting patterns. They used to send her all these drafts of patterns and she had to get to know them and see if they worked out. She'd stand at her gate with all these patterns, trying to work them out. She taught me a lot of things about knitting – that's how I remember her.

Pam Turner (France Lynch)

Left: A portrait of the inimitable local matron Blanche Young, agent for the Children's Society, and the reason why so many orphaned children, such as Harry Cadwallader, were brought to live in Chalford.

Below: A later portrait of Blanche Young and her husband George. He made his own television set and invited Pam Turner and her family to watch the Queen's Coronation in June 1953.

Reverend Richards' good news

We always had a fête of St John the Baptist at France Lynch on 24 June. They used to have teas, but if it rained we were up in the school. There were always little stalls put up on the vicarage lawn and bowling for a pig – my father would invariably give a small pig for the bowling. The Reverend Richards was our vicar at France Lynch. He was the last one that lived in the vicarage. It was very sad – his wife, who was so active and rushing around all over the place, died very suddenly and he himself was very crippled with arthritis. He was a delightful man and he had two sons. One was imprisoned in Singapore and one was in the army. Reverend Richards had to retire due to ill health and he lived up at Bramley opposite the Church Rooms. I can never work out why we did, but I shall never forget when we had a phone call, mother and I, asking if we could we give a message to the Reverend Richards to tell him that his son, Anthony, was on his way home from Singapore. Then they gave a telephone number for him to ring back. I rushed up to Mr Richards to tell him the good news and I said, 'Would you like me to come back in half an hour?' He looked at me and said, 'Thank you. You know, Florence, that news you've brought me, I'm sure I can walk down myself'. He could scarcely walk, but he'd got this wonderful news and in about half an hour he had arrived with two sticks. We sat him down and I couldn't help overhearing what he said on the telephone. I remember Anthony had been imprisoned so long that he didn't know where his brother was and he didn't know his mother had died. Mr Richards had worked out what to say to him, with words from the Bible. He just told Anthony to look up such and such, and such and such in the Bible. Then we had a sit down and a cup of coffee and he said that he could walk back. It was almost like a miracle.

Florence Workman (France Lynch)

Johnny Steel the organist

When I was a child, in about 1938 or 1939, Johnny Steel used to walk by Ashmeads and cut through to Frampton Place by Gassons to go up to Oakridge Church to play the organ. He was a little strange and all the kids would yell out 'Tell us a story, Johnny!' When he played the organ, they put a curtain round him to stop the children making faces at him.

Michael Mills (Chalford)

We used to always have an organist called Johnny Steel. He was quite a character, and once a year they always had a social – like a dance – and a concert and they gave him any money raised from the social. He used to tell a story about a man who had two pairs of glasses and he used to go through a routine taking off one pair of glasses and putting on the other pair. I remember that quite well, because that was through the church and we always went to church.

Pam Turner (France Lynch)

Johnny Steel was a brilliant organist of his day. He lived with some people called Tranter, who were a well-known local family, and they looked after him as he had no family. He was a brilliant organist in his way, but he was a bit scary.

Florence Workman (France Lynch)

The one-legged cobbler...

One of the only shops in Bussage at that time was a small wooden shed just down past the village green on the side of a lane – it's no longer there. It was owned by Mr Phipps, who only had one leg and who used to walk with crutches. But he came from Toadsmoor,

The France Lynch Philomusica Society in the 1920s. This picture features a number of the local characters. From left to right, back row: Blanche Young, Reg Young, Dennis Workman (Florence's brother), Len Blizzard, Ron Blizzard, Mr Marmont, Johnny Steel. Front row: Joan Butler, Keith Jackson, Dolly Davis, Sidney Sharp, Olive Cresswell, Florence Workman, Ron Blizzard, Freda Minchin.

up the hill and past the church, every day and went down every night. He was the cobbler and sold things like paraffin. He'd do all your shoe repairs and, as time progressed and radios became available, he used to charge the accumulators and also sell the high tension batteries. So that was his little niche – he was a very well-known person.

Dave Collins

...and his daughter

Then there was Connie Phipps, who had Down's Syndrome. She was elderly – well, she seemed old to me – and her father was the cobbler from Toadsmoor. She used to get outside the school and she used to shout at us and terrify us. Another time the steamroller was in the village and that petrified me – I was petrified of anything like that.

Kathy Watkins (Brownshill)

A bit of a character

William Banyard, my grandfather, was the gardener at the vicarage and he used to wind the church clock. He lived his little life – he used to go along to the New Inn and have his drink. At that time there were about twelve pubs in Bisley. Women never went – it was only the men. Granny took in washing and ironing – mostly for the vicarage, I think. Grampy worked there for 30s a week. That's all we had to live on and some of that went to the pub. The vicar at the time was called Clay – he had two daughters, Margaret and Ruby. He was quite a strict vicar. He must have been strict with them, but Ruby loved to go out and my grandfather wasn't above putting a ladder up for her to get out the window and go out in the evenings. Grampy wound the clock; in later years, my husband used to have to go up and help him do it once a week, because you had to go quite a way up into the steeple. He was a bell ringer and he used to do the chimes for the services. I did the chimes

Grampy Banyard in full flow at the Bisley Institute with Miss H. Nation at the piano.

once, only once, because he was ill one Sunday. I didn't know music very well, but I could do it because I'd watched him do it so often. Several of us had a go at bell ringing, but it didn't come to anything very much. We used to put on plays for people to come and see up at the WI; there was a stage and the place was packed. We used to sing sometimes, but my grampy used to play the piano. His nickname was Cork, I don't know how he got it. He was a bit of a character. I took part too: mostly I sang.

Muriel Hunt (Bisley)

Sid Barnet from Battlescombe

Sid Barnet used to do a country dance for us sometimes. He was down at Battlescombe – he lived in a caravan down there, but he had no home as such. He was a character – always drinking cider. He was a little bit the worse for drink, very often, but he was a nice man, really. He had no home life and he had no relatives at all, nobody in the world. He'd just do a jog in the street if he felt like it – in wellingtons! Always in wellingtons! You'd never see Sid in anything else other than wellingtons – he'd just sing 'The White Rose of Summer' while he was dancing outside the Stirrup Cup, or the New Inn as it was then.

Hilda Ruther (Bisley)

10 Brownshill
A History of Spiritual Healing

Brownshill, one of the tiny, perched Cotswold villages overlooking the Golden Valley, seems an unlikely place to find a history of spiritual healing and care for the vulnerable stretching back to the mid-nineteenth century. But the same strong Victorian sense of social and moral duty that encouraged Thomas Keble to build churches in the area also brought a young, idealistic vicar to Bussage in 1846.

Robert Suckling was determined to take the Church's message to the poorest and most neglected parts of the country. With so many of his parishioners working long hours in the mills and living in poverty, Suckling had plenty of opportunities to do so in Bussage and Brownshill and he was also chaplain to the Stroud Workhouse, spending time with sick prostitutes on the notorious Black Ward.

Working with Suckling was his neighbour, Grace Anne Poole, a wealthy lady who lived in Brownshill House. Inspired and supported by the Penitentiary Movement, together they opened the House of Mercy, a refuge for repentant prostitutes, at Kirby's Cottage on the slopes of Blackness. Mrs Poole became Mother Superior and her helpers, Sisters of Mercy. Suckling had plans to improve and enlarge the premises, but became ill with typhoid after an outbreak in the village and died, aged only thirty-three years old, in 1851.

Although his death was a severe blow, Mrs Poole and her helpers continued with their work, and when she retired in 1898 and died two years later, the Community of St Mary the Virgin (the Wantage Sisters) took over the running of the home, which they renamed St Michael's Home. The focus changed at this point, taking in young and vulnerable girls who needed protection, some of who were in danger of sliding into prostitution. A laundry was installed to provide the girls with work and the home with an income.

The laundry girls

I was taken to Bussage Church from a month old and I went there for over fifty years. I didn't sing in the choir, but I rang the bell and I belonged to the Sunday School when Revd Barchard was there. We were taken along to the House of Mercy to see the girls do their Christmas and Easter plays. The laundry was made into a little theatre and we sat on these little benches watching the girls in beautiful costumes, which they'd made themselves.

I understood they were girls who had come up against hard times. Reverend Barchard lived in Brownshill House for many years and he was the chaplain to the House of Mercy. I can remember the Sisters bringing the girls along to Bussage Church every Sunday morning: they used to wear raincoats and berets and little black lace-up shoes and they used to come across the fields and you could hear them chattering as they came along the field, but as soon as they got to the road there was no more talking. They would walk down to the church silently and into church. We had the main part of the church with a side aisle where the girls used to sit. They must have had other services in their own chapel there too.

Pam Clissold

Right: *The Reverend Robert Alfred Suckling, born 1818 and vicar of Bussage 1846-51.*

Below: *Brownshill House, home of Grace Poole in the late nineteenth century and later home to Mrs Joan Burns and family.*

The Sisters of the House of Mercy in 1901.

St Raphael's, Brownshill. This was designed by Alban Caroe.

So, the laundry and its girls were already a part of the local community when, coincidentally, in 1923 two extraordinary women, Miss Bertha Kessler and Miss Katherine Hudson, also came to live and work in Brownshill. Both had been nurses during the First World War and, afterwards, had developed their studies in medicine and the social sciences. They had become convinced that mental illness was best treated by a combination of religious faith and accepted methods of psychiatry, and were devising their own programme to help those in the religious community with psychiatric problems.

In 1927, Misses Kessler and Hudson acquired Tanglewood, a late-Victorian house in Brownshill, which they renamed Templewood. Over the next seven years, they admitted female patients, one at a time, to come to live with them and be treated by them. The two women were received into the Catholic faith in 1934 and the following year they built a Catholic church in Brownshill, St Mary of the Angels. They also built St Raphael's, a large house nearby, to provide accommodation for a priest in one of its wings.

The Templewood Home of Rest (or the Brownshill Health Colony) was formed and the operation expanded. Patients lived in small groups within the Community, their daily life run along a simple, religious routine. The Templewood Community bought several cottages, farms and houses and became a substantial property owner in Brownshill and Bussage.

Templewood

There were two maiden ladies in the village who lived at a house called Templewood – Miss Kessler and Miss Hudson. They were very wealthy Roman Catholics. Miss Hudson was very tall, elegant and pale; she was reputed to be related to the 'Hudson Sunlight Soap' family. By comparison, Miss Kessler was of average height, very dark-haired and olive-skinned. I believe she was of Austrian origin and was a Catholic by conversion. I remember her particularly because, for some altruistic

121

reason, she bought a present at Christmas for every child from Brownshill who went to Bussage Church of England School. She not only bought a present, but we were actually asked what we wanted and, if it was within reason, it was purchased. If not, another choice was allowed. I remember the year I was six, I requested a clockwork car with lights – this was my pride and joy – I could hardly bear to leave it alone.

Miss Hudson and Miss Kessler commissioned a church to be built in the early 1930s. It was the first building work I really remember. Then they had a lovely large house built in Cotswold stone which they named St Raphael's. They also acquired Vine Farm at the other end of Brownshill village. Then they started to colonise Brownshill and Bussage by buying quality houses as they became vacant. These houses were occupied by women who dressed mainly in nuns' raiment – what their purpose in life was, I never gave a thought. They employed several men and women with learning disabilities to do menial and farm work and a manager to run the farm, together with several local women who cooked and cleaned for them. I went to the big house called Templewood once with a friend whose mother worked there and witnessed the novelty of the first vacuum cleaner I had ever seen. I remember being allowed to rip up several bits of paper and watch them being sucked up by the noisy machine. There were always two or three priests in residence and they were very pleasant fellows, especially Father Ryan, who was quite a popular character.

George Gleed (Brownshill)

In 1936, men, mainly priests, began to be admitted for treatment as well as women. But in 1946, a plane crashed into Templewood and completely destroyed the house. The work with men was then dramatically scaled down until 1959, when the Servants of the Paraclete, an American order which supports priests in need of psychiatric care, came to Firwood House in Brownshill, having heard about and met Miss Kessler and Miss Hudson.

A plane crash

I remember after the war in 1946, there was a plane crash – a Lancaster bomber taking off from Aston Down on a training flight got into difficulties. In trying to get back it came very low over Eastcombe, clipped a tree in a wood over Brownshill and eventually crashed into a house there. I was about twelve. I was at Marling but I was off ill with an ear infection; Dad was off ill too, so we were both at home fed up with everything. A crash was a real interest. It happened late morning, and I remember going over early afternoon to see the devastation. The house that was destroyed was called Tanglewood, (renamed Templewood by Miss Kessler and Miss Hudson). It was a very nice stone-built house. It was never rebuilt. Later on, Dad was employed by a Catholic community in Brownshill. This house had never been rebuilt, and when I was building my house, I was looking for some stone and I asked him if he would ask the owners of Templewood if I could go along and scavenge. So, in the 1960s, that's exactly what I did. Templewood is still a pile of stones.

David Collins (Bussage)

While working on Dad's bungalow one day, we heard a low aircraft which came overhead and just missed us. It crashed on Templewood in Brownshill, which was one of the lovely houses belonging to the Catholics and, for some reason, has never been re-built. I think the aircraft was a Lancaster bomber, from which I saw four bodies being carried away. I remember Brother John, who was in the house, was burned badly.

George Gleed (Brownshill)

PLANE CRASHES INTO NURSING HOME. CREW KILLED, PATIENTS' MIRACULOUS ESCAPES

A four-engined aircraft, believed to be a Lancaster, crashed into the side of Templewood Nursing Home at Brownshill at about a quarter past eleven yesterday morning, killing the crew of the plane and injuring one of the occupants of the home.

Both the plane and the building burst into flames. Occupants of the house at the time had miraculous escapes from serious injury and only one person was injured. Mr John Adams, who was taken to the Gloucester City General Hospital, was suffering from severe burns and injuries to his back.

Early yesterday afternoon two bodies had been recovered from the wreckage of the plane. It is believed there was a third occupant of the plane. Those killed were Squadron Leader R.H. Thomas and Flight Sergeant Gray.

Fire appliances attended from Stroud, Nailsworth and Cirencester and within an hour had the fire in the house under control, but very little remained of the building except the outer walls. Pieces of the plane were strewn over a considerable distance, and it was completely destroyed. The fire-fighting operations were in the charge of Company Officer R.F .Taylor.

The noise of the explosion could be heard as far away as Minchinhampton and police, under Inspector Herbert, were quickly on the scene.

The occupants of Templewood at the time of the crash were: Mr John Adams of Hermit Cottage, Father Philip Darnley, Father Clark, Mr Ewen Cameron, Mrs Savery and Mrs Davies.

EYE WITNESS STORIES

Father Philip Darnley climbed out of a bedroom window and escaped down a drainpipe to safety. The other four occupants of the house were uninjured and managed to extricate themselves. The residents at Templewood were Miss Kessler, Father Darnley and three patients, Father Madden, Father Clark and Father Reynolds. Fortunately, three of the residents were out of the house at the time of the crash.

Miss Kessler said: 'I was in the Post Office, and as I was coming out I saw the plane fly very low over my head. I lost sight of it but, arriving within view of the house, I saw it had crashed and both the plane and the house were burning furiously.'

A Roman Catholic priest said 'I was working in my study at my home higher up the hillside, when I heard a plane come over which apparently had engine trouble. I heard an explosion and, running out, saw that the nursing home was on fire and flames were also coming from the plane which had crashed in front of the house.

Mrs T Furley of Brownshill said that she heard a plane flying low close to the house, but did not take much notice as many planes often flew over the district. The plane came very close to the house and a moment later she heard a tremendous crash and huge quantities of smoke came up from just below her house. All the windows in the house shook. 'It seemed to happen in a split second,' declared Mrs Furley.

The gardener at the home, Mr Charlie Wood, gave a graphic description of how he was near the greenhouse in the garden of the house at the time and heard the plane coming. The plane seemed to break into three pieces and fall on part of the house. A few moments later he saw the house go up in flames. He saw Father Philip Darnley, who was in the house at the time, climb out of a bedroom window and down a drainpipe.

Another eye-witness told our representative that he saw the plane flying shortly before the accident coming from the Bisley direction and that it just missed two houses at Frith Wood. Making south, it collided with a tree in College Wood and the tail of the plane fell off. About a quarter of a mile further on it crashed into Templewood. Several people who heard the plane flying low stated that the engines appeared to be 'missing' shortly before the accident.

Stroud News and Journal,
Friday 15 March 1946.

Brother John stands outside Templewood in the early 1930s.

We came to live in Brownshill House

When my husband Peter got home from the war, we came up to live in Brownshill House and met the two ladies who'd started the Templewood Community, Miss Hudson and Miss Kessler, and we were asked to lunch. They belonged to the Dominicans, but they were not vowed nuns. They were dedicated women who wore a nylon overall and a headscarf and if they were in the community they wore a belt. The final Sister, Philomena, who became the leader after the two founders died, came from Australia and she only died the year before last.

Joan Burns (Brownshill)

St Michael's Home, the laundry, closed in 1947. It was then used temporarily as a boys' home and then an old people's home until finally the Servants of the Paraclete moved there from Firwood House.

Refurbished and renamed Our Lady of Victory, the old laundry is today a games room and the chapel there has been enlarged. The Servants of the Paraclete have created a home of peace and prayer and a regime of rest and recovery which is, after all, in keeping with its history and true to the memory of the original founders, the Reverend Suckling and Grace Poole, to whom a memorial plaque hangs in the entrance hall.

In 1963, Miss Kessler and Miss Hudson died within three weeks of one another and were succeeded by Sister Philomena Murray. The women's Community became the Little Company

The Catholic church at Brownshill, dedicated to St Mary of the Angels in 1937. The church was built on the site of an old barn in the village which was reputed to contain stones from an Anglo-Saxon chapel.

of Hope. However, as a result of government policy, changes in attitudes to mental health and other external forces, fewer female patients were coming to Brownshill and, eventually, in 1996, Sister Philomena was the only member living at St Raphael's. The Community was forced to sell off some of its properties, offering them to other religious communities. St Raphael's became the home of the Congregation of Mary, Mother of the Church, to whom Sister Philomena handed over the responsibilities of the Little Company of Hope. She died in 1997 at the age of eighty-nine and is buried near her predecessors at St Mary of the Angels.

Other Gloucestershire titles published by Tempus

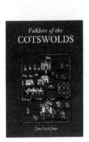

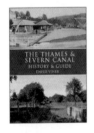

If you are interested in purchasing other books published by Tempus, or in case you have difficulty finding any Tempus books in your local bookshop, you can also place orders directly through our website

www.tempus-publishing.com

or from   **BOOKPOST**, Freepost, PO Box 29, Douglas, Isle of Man, IM99 1BQ
tel 01624 836000   email bookshop@enterprise.net